A Cowboy's Wisdom

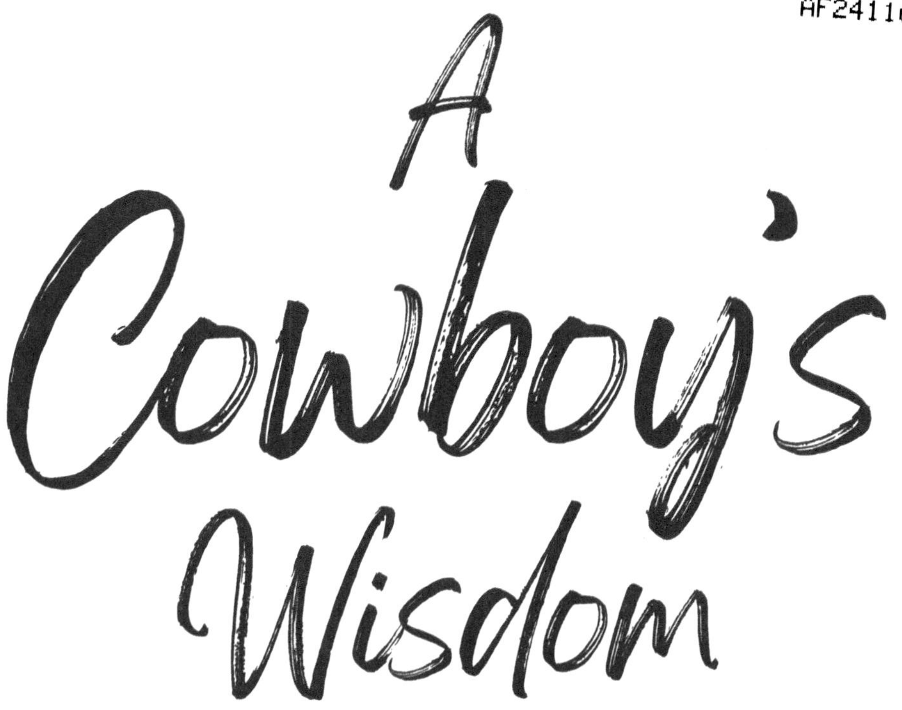

MARK HAYWOOD

LEADERSHIP
Thoughtful, Relevant Leaders From Around The World
BOOKS

Dedication

I DEDICATE THIS BOOK TO a man who was raised in a small town and set himself above the rest early in life. At an incredibly early age, he worked two jobs, one before school and the other after, to help the financial needs of his family. He helped support his younger brother and two sisters. His mom worked on the farm and sewed for anyone who asked, and together they made ends meet. It became obvious that helping his family brought him more joys than burdens as his grades excelled and he was voted in as president of his Senior Class. His efforts in school, church, and his home life shined in the community to the point where a kind member of their church saw to it that he received tuition for his first year of college. This help kickstarted his success in college which concluded with a master's degree. It also led to passing the CPA Exam and a career that took him up the ladder to the position of Vice President of the University of North Florida, which he held until his retirement after 33 years of service in the university system.

Throughout his life, his heart was burdened with concern for others. Whether it was his own family as a young man, classmates in high school, or his small town, he kept an eye out for others who might need a hand from a friend. As time passed, he raised a family with his bride, Mary Ester Brooks, who he loved dearly, and together, they raised a family with two girls and two boys. The direction of his concern transformed into helping lead and teach others. He had a deep love for teaching others.

Throughout the many years I have known the man, and the many years I saw him show genuine love for others, I am certain our Lord had His hand on him. I know without a doubt that the Lord ordained him for a special purpose, for he impacted the lives of more people than we will ever know. I do know of one preacher that this man impacted to the point of changing his life and destiny. I credit him as the man who God used to direct my path to teach God's word. This gentleman that I speak so highly of is Mr. Jim Carlton Haywood, my dad.

Table of Contents

Preface

WHILE YOU READ THROUGH THE pages of this little book you will find daily ponderings of all types. There are multitudes of life situations that have found their way into each century and generation. These situations are found in most every family or individual's life. There are some challenges that are regional problems that have affected the community. Finally, you will find cowboy poetry that will swoon the hardest of cowboy's hearts. A wise man many years ago said, "there was nothing new under the sun." This book seems to prove him out. Each of life's challenges, both good and bad, finds its participants seeking the wisest and clearest of answers. One of the main characters within these pages is a rural cowboy pastor. As he is brought to each dilemma, while talking it through, the Rural Cowboy Pastor is able to show the relevance of Scripture.

When something is broken or not working like it should, it is always best to seek out wisdom from its creator or the manual the creator wrote to help you along the way. God left us such a manual in the Scriptures. Although sometimes it may not be easy to find your answer written its pages in either black or red, your answer is there. Jesus even shared with us in His life that He suffered in every way that we have, and He was tempted in every way. This gives us a Lord and Savior that we truly can run to in every situation, knowing that He understands, and He cares.

So, will you ride along with this cowboy and let him show you the relevance of Scripture in every situation you may find yourself in? Further, knowing that God loves you and so do I.

Introduction

STRESS, STRUGGLES, AND HARDSHIPS CANNOT be avoided in life; they may even be a part of life itself. A child may feel them all while moving though the birthing canal. His lungs fill up with oxygen for the very first time, and his blood carries that oxygen throughout his body. The nerves awake and come alive. There's that first *"whack"* across the rear pain, and hardships begin.

In today's world, where men are dressing up as women and parading themselves through town, where your child must have a parent's permission slip before going to afternoon "show and tell" at school. This world has truly turned upside down. It seems left is right, and right is wrong. Each day you think you have figured things out, they change the rules on you again. Whether at work, home, or play, there is nowhere you can relax and just be yourself.

With the struggles in today's world, from the political to the private, how are we to keep our sanity? Well now, that was quite a bold statement. If you have a left-sided political worldview, and the personal side of your life is rolling along just as you planned it, then you are probably a very happy camper. However, if you have a right-sided/conservative worldview, and your life is not going along like God planned it, you're probably, as some would say, feeling "slap torn apart".

Inside this little book, along with the ones that follow, are principles and truths that are as simple as a cowboy's wisdom, and they can help guide you to peace. The complications that have you all tied up in knots can be untied. The relationships that have been broken or are at this very moment being torn apart can be repaired. This crazy, mixed-up world can be made right, and the part that is affecting you can be peaceful.

Take a few moments each morning and read a tale. Let an ole cowboy share some truths that have helped people for thousands of years. For it is the life of the cowboy where you find simplicity. It is in the life of the Christian cowboy that you can find peace.

God loves you, and so do I,

Pastor Mark Haywood

Freeze!

WHEN THINKING OF THE COWBOY, my generation might think of Robert Redford in the movie *The Horse Whisperer*. He portrayed a man that was humble and was always there for his neighbor. He saw to the needs of his family and did his best at teaching the kids about God's beauty in nature.

That beauty in nature is a relationship that we have with all things. Our relationship with our spouse, our children, our neighbors, and all of God's creation. The most important is with our Lord Jesus. When we take note of how easy it is to live out the Kingdom of God, you see kingdom living is simple. It is other-centered. I believe it is the basis of the Cowboy Code. It is relationship-based and has nothing to do with religion.

Make it your lifestyle, your way of livin'. Let's show the world why being a cowboy is the best way.

God loves you, and so do I.

Hope

A PERSON LIVING DAY TO day without hope, not knowing what tomorrow will bring nor how he will pay for it, must live an awful life. Each day on the news, all we hear is war. A war starting out in Ukraine being attacked by Russians now has countries across Europe and even the United States getting involved.

That person without hope was finally getting over the fight of the COVID-19 Pandemic. Now he is having to fear if we are going to war. Is Russia going to be firing bombs at us? What should he be doing to prepare and keep himself and his family safe? Hope? That person only dreams of having some.

Possibly you are like me, and you have a hope living inside you. To explain it thoroughly is almost impossible. We just know that it is there. I know that it does not matter the degree of the challenges, my hope is always there and never leaves me.

My hope is found in my faith in Jesus Christ. How about you? What do you lean on when life comes crashing down. Our world is in turmoil. Our states and families are in disarray. Our children do not have heroes and leaders in their homes to look up to and they only cry out for hope.

Would you please share my messages with others? Even better will you do as I do and share with others where and in who you have hope?

God loves you, and so do I.

After Cussing He Quit!

WHILE OUT SITTING BY HIS campfire, the old cowboy was working with his ropes. He had picked up a couple new ones when he was in town last, and they were stiff as a bone. He could never figure out why they came that way. You couldn't lasso a fence post while they were in that condition. So, there he sat bending and twisting while rubbing in some saddle soap until he felt they were worth using.

If you and I could have seen the cowboy and the way he attacked those ropes, I do believe we could have told that the ropes were not the only thing he was working out.

The way the story was told, while the cowboy was sitting by his fire, he heard someone calling to him. It was not that of just any man and it was not just any voice. The cowboy turned side to side and saw no one. The voice kept calling, "Drop your ropes son and ride with me. I will turn you into a gatherer of strays."

The cowboy did just that. It was said that he just left his old ways there next to that campfire and started following Jesus. For three years the cowboy rode across some of the hardest terrain telling folks about Christ and leading them to salvation.

Until one day.

He rode into a town early in the morning and started inviting the people to join him that afternoon. He told them that he would be telling them things that would change their lives if they would just come and listen.

That afternoon as the crowd started to gather the cowboy noticed a group of fellas that looked familiar. They were a group of ruff neck cowboys from his past.

These fellas came up on him from out of nowhere. Pushing and shoving as they threatened to tell the crowd what a hypocrite he was. They were going to tell them about how he would lie, cheat, and drink his way through every dance hall that side of the delta.

Things got really bad as the people in the crowd started to believe the roughnecks, and they turned on him. It was said that the cowboy started cussing and threw his Bible into the crowd as he rode off. It was there sitting at his campfire he started mumbling, "I quit. I ain't doing this no more."

I am told that some time that night the cowboy heard that same voice. But this time the voice said, "Don't worry about them ropes son. Let 'em lay were they fall. Saddle up and ride with me and I teach you to gather strays the right way."

Folks, if some time in your past you accepted Jesus as your savior and now you find yourself doing things you are not proud of. Maybe it's booze, drugs, or just living life without Him, Jesus is still there. He is still asking you to let Him help you. Maybe it's time you laid it down and rode with Him.

God loves you, and so do I.

Christian Cowboys

IT WAS AN EARLY START to my day. The moon was still hidden from the morning sky, and the sun had yet to shine its light on my path. I was saddled up on my favorite mare and riding in to meet the fellas at the Diner. The horse was taking the center of the road so as not to kick up or to stumble over a stone in her path. She centers on knowing my every move and desire. I feel as if I could drop my reins knowing she would take me right to breakfast. Laying back in my saddle, I could feel the coolness of the morning's dawn on my skin. I didn't realize it, but I had dozed off, and as I awoke, I tilted my hat just enough to see the embers of the morning sunlight come across the fields of golden grain. The joy that filled my heart was indescribable.

Once I arrived at the Diner, most of the fellas were out front. I glanced over each of their faces, and it seemed every one of us was having the same experience. We all had that look. You know the one. That look you get right after you just know you have seen God today. Who knows, maybe we all had.

I paid close attention as each one made their way inside the main door to the Diner. I heard phrases such as "Excuse me, ma'am", "Good morning," and "How do you do?" Once inside, they hung up their hats while saying hello or howdy to any and all that were in the room. The freedom and joy that only Christ can give is expressed on the face of only a Christian. You could almost feel it as they looked you in your eyes, and with a big smile and a polite greeting, the fellas filled the place with warmth and kindness.

The Christian cowboy is a person that may or may not have even touched a cow nor saddled up a horse, but they have a country mindset. They see beauty in all the nature that God created. They've allowed God to change them – helping them to be more concerned about others than they are about themselves.

One day, while walking and talking with His disciples Jesus was thinking about The Law of Moses. He was wondering how to break it down in such a way that even a cowboy could understand. Jesus realized the Law was impossible for man to follow exactly, for it was there to point out to man his sin. I can imagine Jesus there with a big grin on his face, thinking I will give them something they can call "Christianity for even cowboys". He said, "Fellas, love God with all your heart and love your neighbor as yourself." There you have it.

To be a Christian is to acknowledge that you are a work in progress. By allowing the Holy Spirit to work in and through you on a daily basis, your goal to be more like Christ will become focused and habitual. That is a good habit to have.

Saddle up, cowboys. Let's all ride for the brand. The JC brand.

God loves you, and so do I.

It's Their Fault!

BACK AT THE RANCH THIS time of year we are preparing the ground for the garden. Then there is still putting out hay bales and cubes for the cattle. Oh, we all know how the horses are about getting into trouble. It seems every cowboy gets worn out even more this time of year.

Fighting back the cold and the snow getting wet all makes it harder to get the job finished. Then there's the mud you try to drive through and sometimes find yourself stuck. Walking around in the heavy snow or mud sometimes just wears you out and when you finally make it home two hours late you hear "where have you been?"

"Where have you been?" Really, after all you've been through. She says I have had supper waiting now for two hours and the kids must go to bed. Not to mention I must help them with their homework. I have had to clean this house and now you are tracking in all that mud and have messed it up and I still have supper ready for you and you don't even show. What are you thinking? I am so tired of this. Tomorrow I am feeding me and the kids, and you will be on your own.

Has anything like this ever happened to you?

In Genesis, when God came to Adam about the eating of the forbidden fruit, Adam blamed it on the women He gave him. Then Eve blamed it on the "devil made me do it." It is referred to as escape avoidance.

As Christians, the opportunity or the desire to blame should not even rise to the surface. With the Holy Spirit living inside us, the old man or sinful man has been put to death and the new man is alive thanks to Christ Jesus. This does not mean we will not struggle, but we have the ability to look to others needs. We should be other-centered, not self-centered.

In your relationships with others, regardless of if it's at home, work, or play, how are you perceived? Are you a woman or a man who is able to share the love of Christ after a tense situation? Remember even after Jesus was beaten and crucified for false reasons, He still said Father forgive them.

God loves you, and so do I.

Jackie Edwards

THE FOLLOWING PEARL OF WISDOM was given to me by my dear friend and wonderful sister in our Lord, Mrs. Jackie Edwards. Jackie is one of the strongest and wisest women in Christ that I know. She has been a friend, an encourager, and a confidant of mine for many years. When Jackie shared this piece with me I was proud to add it in this book. I'm sure you too will benefit from her wisdom shared as I have.

"Being positive in a negative world is difficult even for the best of God's children. It seems each day has its own challenges. We can get up happy and ready for the day, but by night, we are just plain ol' tuckered out. For married people, it's even more complicated. Trying to not take out what happened in our day on our spouse can be difficult.

The key word that has somehow got lost in all the minutiae of a day's trials is communication. That's when husband and wife, parents and children, or whatever the combination is, sit down and talk about their day and why they feel the way they do. Each person who is not talking is listening with love, understanding, and compassion. Not sitting in judgement and making unkind comments. At the end of the conversation, each person has had a chance to explain their day and why they feel the way they do, and a chance to listen and sympathize with the others. It's called God's love, and it is the best equalizer there is.

If we can listen and sympathize with a frazzled person and allow them to have their feelings, they are going to be more ready to do the same for you when it's your turn to talk. Real honest, humble, communicating is the ultimate showing of God's love because you make each other really feel like you care about their feelings. The love it generates in a family is amazing, and everyone feels validated about their feelings and who they are! It's a win-win, and if you do it enough, it heads off hurt feelings, before they have a chance to get hurt. Being selfless, in a self-centered world, is as easy as you make it, because it is so worth it! I wish someone would have told me this when I was young and trying to raise children, with a hard to get along with husband.

Maybe it would have saved my marriage. I hope as you read this it might save you the heartache of a broken home!

God bless you all!"

Is There a Real Man Out There?

OUR COUNTRY FACES MORE CHALLENGES today than ever. Our state is troubled with mistrust in leadership. Crime is on the rise in cities and towns. Families are having to function without Dads. Fathers are leaving the mothers of their children. Children are having to grow up without not only the affection of their dad, but they are going without the skills that a dad should have taught them. Dads should be teaching their children by way of example things like how to treat a woman, how to be a husband and how to earn and hold the respect as a father and how to pass it on to their children. There are things outside the home, such as the role a man holds in the culture and community. A man should show his children why unity is so important in the home and how the principle rolls out into the community and country. This principle starts by teaching the children to follow rules in the home. Then the same principle should roll out to obey the Laws in the community and the Country

Real Men where are you?

Yes, there are plenty of men to be found. There are "Baby-Daddies" and there are "Real Men."

Some would say, "Well, preacher, I married her and have stayed with the family all these years. Even that does not make you a "Real Man".

I would answer, "That may be true. The family may have had a male adult, but did they have a real man to lead them?"

Any cowboy can jump on a horse and ride, but it takes a real man, I would go as far as to say a Christian Cowboy to saddle up and run a Ranch.

God asked the question: "Adam, where are you?"

Adam was hiding in the garden using leaves to cover himself. Specifically, Adam was in the home wrapping himself with goods he could find, hiding from all the responsibilities God gave him.

So, you see, men can be hiding today at work, in the church, and in their homes. They can cover themselves with all the nice things and names they can find, but they are running from the responsibilities they have as leaders, dads and real men.

Adam, where are you?

God loves you, and so do I.

A Brother From a Mother of Another Color

IT WAS EARLY ONE SUNDAY morning. The boys and I had been out rounding cattle all week. But it was Sunday. We all gathered under an ole oak, and each of us broke out our Bibles safely secured in our saddlebags.

Now there were 10 of us cowboys, all from the Double R ranch. We had known one another going on 10 years. Working the cowboy life, getting to know one another, really doesn't quite define it. Cowboying is a risky job. When you roll up your night roll and strap it down to your saddle each morning, you really don't know if you are going to make it back in one piece. Sometimes you aren't sure if you will make it back at all. Each Cowboy has to be able to rely on the others. When bringing a herd back and you find yourself facing off a wild bull, you have to instinctively know where the other cowboys are and know they will be there for you if you need a hand.

This trip, the boys and I were out rounding up strays. Mostly wild, all cantankerous, and not a one coming along gently. It did not matter the job; every Sunday we always took time to give thanks to God for our safety, our cattle, and our families back home. We didn't really have a preacher of sorts. So, we would each take turns reading the Word, saying what we felt the Good Lord was placing on our hearts, and then wrapping it up with prayer. This day was different. The lesson the Lord would teach us did not come from anything we had read. Nor was it expected. As I said, there we all were, and I believe it was my turn to lead. I had just started reading Genesis Chapter 2 when I heard one of the fellas say, "What in the world." Now, thinking he was talking about something I had read, I looked deeper at the words. I did not think I had misread anything. But no. Then the rest of the fellas started.

"Look."

I turned, and there they were. We had heard stories; I mean who had not. As kids we were told about these people that were brought over to America on slave ships. They said they were from Africa or places like that. Anyway, they were dark-skinned people. It's just that we had never seen one. There must have been twenty or so and they were riding up on our camp. We really did not know what to do. I mean what could we do? When they came up and asked if it was the Bible we were reading, I said, "Yes, you know of God's Bible." They all agreed and asked to join in our worship time. Well, after that day was over, not only had we made some good friends, but we all learned a valuable lesson.

A couple of us from the Double R talked later that night. We sadly recalled another bunch of folks who, like our new friends, had been severely mistreated. If you ask me, based on my limited knowledge, this other group was treated even worse. The group I speak of did not have white skin like us nor dark like our new friends but were of a red color. They called themselves "The People of the Land". They too, were held captive, bound, and treated as slaves. However, unlike our new friends, they were forced to live, work, and die on the very soil they at one time called their own.

It was not until later that our United State Government decided to round them up like cattle and force them to live out their days on a rocky soiled reservation. Physically the two groups were probably just as horribly mistreated. It was inwardly of the heart that I speak of. This later group came to be known as the American Indian.

If you cannot tell by now, the lessons taught us that day were about judging one another. Every woman, man and child has been created in the image of God and was formed by God Himself. He knows each of us down to the number of hairs on our head. Scripture says He calls us by name, and yet, He was willing to die for every one of us. Scripture says that there is no greater love that one has for another than one being willing to lay down His life for the other. There are days that I have to ask myself, "What am I willing to do for someone else?" How about you?

God loves you, and so do I.

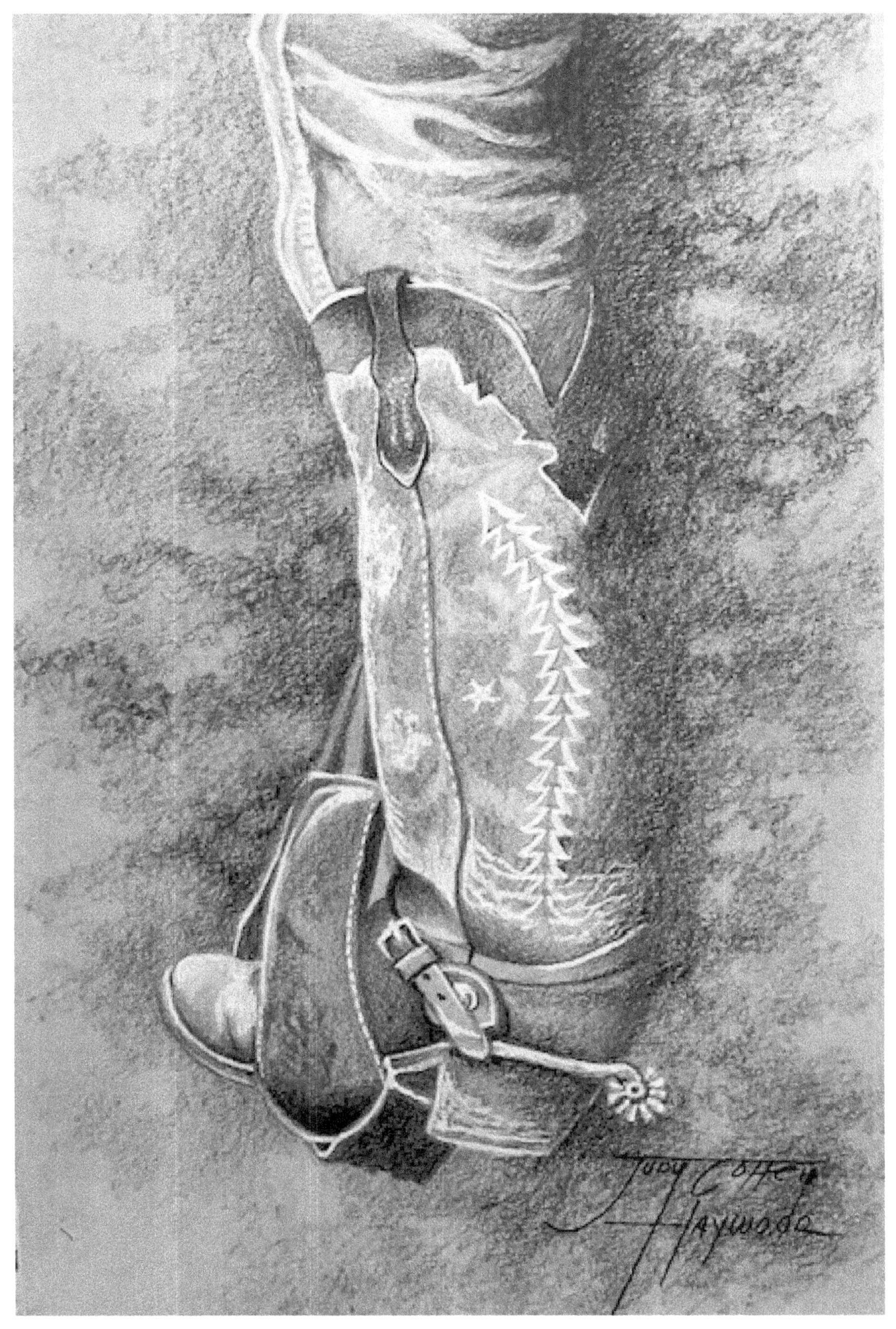

Chocolate Cake, Candy, Ice Cream

WHAT IS IT YOU LOVE?

You might hear things like this from friends or your family. Maybe, you have said, man I love ... whatever noun you want to place at the end of that sentence. The word *love* has come to have several meanings. We say we love our spouse. We say we love our children, and we might love our home. Each time the word love has a different meaning. So, what is love?

In 1st John, John the apostle tells us God is love, and God has been here way before you or I or even all of creation was here. God loved Himself prior to anything. Himself? Yes, God the Father loved the Son, and the Son loved the Holy Spirit and so on. If we are to know love, we must come to know God.

In a complete expression of God, the Father's love for the Son He created mankind to praise and honor the Son through the Holy Spirit. To be sure the honor and praise was complete, God gave freewill to mankind so that each person has the choice to choose Jesus or not. By giving mankind freedom, it opened the door for Satan to place the thought that we do not need God in our head, keeping us outside of God's love. This was sin.

For those who choose to love the Son and receive the love of the Father through the act and sacrifice of his son, you will be giving true praise and honor to Him and return the love to God. We must remember God has asked us to also love one another.

In the family of God, *love* is to decide, regardless emotion, to compassionately seek the betterment of another.

God loves you.

Do you love God?

Are you expressing that love by loving one another? Scripture says we are known by our love.

God loves you, and so do I.

What's On Your Mind Today?

AS FOR ME, I AM not sure if it is concern or a little bit of fear. People are saying we are nearing the end of the world. Some say that Jesus himself is coming back real soon. Others are claiming that the works of man have destroyed everything we touch and now the consequences are starting. The Earth is going to explode. Most people when hearing something like this cry out to God. It is like the person drowning, and they are going under the water for the last time, and you cry, "God help me".

Running to God, people begin to pray (the best they know how) or they pick up a Bible or look on Google to find a word or two they can hold on too for some peace. Speakers all over the world are preaching their understanding of the end.

Sermons proclaiming that the end as you know it is coming. Some of these sermons enter a deep theological debate that we will not come to a clear understanding of this side of life.

I heard a sermon today about the "Unforgettable Sin." Now there is a new fear for you to consider.

What about the average Joe? The person that is trying to just make it through the end of the day. He hopes the choices he has made will bring him some profit. He hopes he will experience some joy and if he comes across another in need, he hopes he will be able to help that person a little. But mainly he wants to have enough for his own family he does not expect life will give him more than what he may need for that day.

I wonder what the average Joe thinks about this fear of the end of time. Maybe he just pushes it aside and does not think about it at all. But not thinking about it does not make it go away. What is the average Joe hearing and who is telling him?

Christians are told to go out and tell others about the good news, the Gospel. By sharing the good news, we are sharing the truth of what is going on, and we share the only way for the average Joe to escape the horrors to come and can have peace and joy for eternity. If told in an uninformed way, it will sound too good to be true. The average Joe? What does he think when he hears this?

I believe the scriptures. I believe each word to be true and from God Himself. I am positive that every person has sinned, and they need a Savior. I believe that Jesus Christ is the only way to receive forgiveness of the wrongs we have done, and through Jesus, one will find salvation. It is through Jesus we can find the only way to Heaven. It is Heaven where you will find the peace, joy, and love we seek.

If you are an "Average Joe" and you have a question about this, please feel free to write to me. I will explain to you the truth from the Word of God.

What's on your mind today?

God loves you, and so do I.

One to Think About

I HAVE BEEN A READER, member, and or poster on LinkedIn for many years. It seems the longer time passes the more I am reading ads that promote Christian theology classes, getting your Christian degree, and wonderful growth among a higher-level learner. Then too, I have read several articles on the deprived lifestyle of some nonbelievers. These are fewer but more and more extreme. Each of these articles are written for the "wow" factor. You know, get your story out there loud and proud for shock value.

I wonder, am I just missing those articles that explain Biblical terminology or the Biblical Culture. You know the ones that explain things to the average Joe or maybe there just have not been any and those that we do read are just discussing a "preacher's verbal battle" or as it was known back when I was in Seminary "Cognitive Calisthenics." Therefore, the Average Joe, you probably know many of them. Maybe a believer. He and his 2.5 kids and wife have a small home in the suburbs. They try to go to church each Sunday. Both Joe and his wife hold a job, and it takes every bit of their salaries to make ends meet. The kids are in school going through the pressures of studies and the social problem of being with all their friends. No major problems here, just living life.

Where are the articles of encouragement for Joe and his wife? College, I'm not sure if either of them went, but if they didn't, who's got the time or money to afford to go now? As I stated it takes every time, they must keep food on the table and clothes on the kids back. It seems those kids are growing out of things as quick as the outfits are purchased. Where are the articles that tell Joe and his wife everything is going to be, ok? Hope, trust, and love are three words that still exist and have true meaning.

Where is the man or woman who are not seeking fame or gain but just want to extend a hand?

Like I said, maybe I've just overlooked them. Just one to think about.

God loves you, and so do I.

Hey! What is That on the Bottom of Your Boots?

ONE DAY WHILE OUT WORKING the calves, Jack and I were walking in it for hours if you know what I mean. Hour after hour, I guess the stuff just got deeper. Now Jack stayed in the pin while I jumped up on my horse and ran outside the pin chasing a stray. This changed the look of the bottom of my boots. Mine had time to dry and knocked off some of the stuff Jack and I were standing in. Good ole Jack's boots, his were freshly soiled.

Come midafternoon, Jack and I stopped for a cup of coffee. I had a good fire blazing as Jack came up out of the pit. Coffee was coming to a boil, and man, we both needed it. Jack grabbed the cups out of his saddle bag, and I poured the coffee.

It seemed we just sat down as a few of our neighbors came riding by. I said howdy while I noticed ole Jack had turned his head and made himself busy so he would not have to speak. I asked him why he would do such a thing. I asked him if he had any issues with any of the neighbors. He said no. He just would rather not deal with them.

Jack, don't you remember what we talked about in church Sunday? Jesus simplified everything down for cowboys like you and me. He said to love God with all your heart, soul, and mind. Then He said we were to love our neighbors as ourselves. This means to forgive them, to pray for them, and even to help them with whatever needs they may have. Nothing nor less than you would do for yourself.

Friends, as you and I walk out our lives telling folks that we are Christians, let's make sure we act like it. From the tips of our head to the soles of our feet. As you smile and greet folks today, what are you hiding at the bottom of the soles of your feet?

Should Christians Celebrate Valentine's Day?

VALENTINE'S DAY IS A DAY to honor a couple of faithful martyrs. St. Valentines was put to death for his faith It was reported, he restored the sight of a young girl prior to his martyrdom. It was on the day he was to be killed that he sent her a letter signed, "your Valentines." From here, the Church encouraged celebrating and honoring the saints that were put to death for their faith. Later, the day's celebration turned to the giving of greeting cards and gifts to those special in people's lives.

Now, even though Valentine's Day is not some kind of a national holiday, it is a national feast day in the Anglican Church.

Should Christians celebrate? Yes. More directly, I feel that Christian men should daily do as it is written in 2nd Peter where we are told Abram constantly lifted Sara up as a queen. Guys, if you want your wives to follow your leadership at home, be a leader that she will want to follow. Ladies, don't forget your husbands have a very large ego, and he needs you to be his number one cheerleader. He chose you as one to love, the one that he holds in highest regard, and he needs to know that you have taken just a few moments to do something special for him. Show him how much you appreciate him. Even today, write him a note and when you do sign it, "Your Valentine."

Christians, to have a special day once a year to go out of your way for someone you love and appreciate is an exceptionally good thing, yet it would be Christ-like to do this all year long. God loves you, and so do I.

Truth With a Twist

"TRUTH WITH A TWIST WILL make straight your way to Hell."

Last night, just as my bride and I were about to lie down for the night's rest, I received a call. It was not from anyone that I knew, but it was from someone that I had received the same greeting from once before. I remembered because it was a greeting with a touch of sarcasm. He said "Hello." I replied, "Hello." Then I heard with a very sarcastic ear, "A preacher I presume." To which I replied, "Correct." From there, the conversation sounded more like a discussion in a sophomoric class in philosophy, with its deep underlying tones and hidden meanings. Until I was told, "I am a born-again believer. I was raised southern Baptist and was saved." To which I jumped in and quickly responded, "How do you get saved?"

The philosophical answers were over. Now he had to tell me what he thought was truth. The answer I received was "You must believe that God sent his son to save the world and through our faith our works will be found righteous." He went on to quote James His Apostle. "Faith without Works is dead.".

This man had been deceived. Someone had taken a little bit of Scripture and turned it into a lie.

"Truth twisted with lies to the point it has become a lie."

Oh, my goodness, Lord.

Yes, God did love the world so much He sent His son, His only son, to die a horrible death as payment for our sins. If anyone would just believe in Him, they would be saved from the penalty of sin.

Nowhere in the Bible is there a portion whereby mankind must work to earn his salvation. If that was true. At what point would you know that you were Saved? You say you are good. How do you know if you are good enough? Since we have a sinful nature. You would never. More sin would require more work. Further, you have sinned against an eternal God, and therefore, you owe an eternal payment. Only an eternal God could pay an eternal price.

This trick of Satan has been brought to light. He uses just enough truth to draw you into his twist. It is here that you miss the mark and make your way straight to Hell.

I have such good news for you. Neither yours nor my salvation relies on any work we do. Jesus did it all! All we must do is believe in him. Our salvation is a gift.

Let's take some time today thanking Him for our gift of salvation. Then, let's pray for those who fall for Satan's twisted trap.

God loves you, and so do I.

Christianity for Dummies

JUST AFTER WAKING UP AND having my usual Sunday morning fight with Satan wanting me to stay in bed, I got up and made it out of the house and down to the barn. I called in my horse and saddled him up, all along feeling hesitant about wanting to go to church at all. I really was not looking forward to all the backbiting and negative talk. Nor hearing the people snapping off about one thing or another.

I was sure not looking forward to those that put on their imaginary church clothes and church smiles. I'm sure some of you know what I mean. They make themselves out to be Jesus's best friend when I know who they are come Monday.

Oh, as your pastor, how these weigh so heavy on my shoulders. As I rode into town all along praying, *Father, did I correctly understand the message you have for your people?* After making it to the Church house, I only speak to those who see me. Because my goal is to get alone in my office.

Once in my office, God revealed this to me. It is so simple, and it is strong, and it is so true.

CHRISTIANITY FOR DUMMIES

LOVE GOD WITH ALL YOUR HEART AND
EACH OTHER AS YOU DO YOURSELF.

Jesus gave us the answer when He told us:

Love God and love people. That includes yourself

If you're not the type to read about the ceremonies and all the laws in Scripture. Some people just are not the reading kind of folks. But even if you are. It can be tuff. So Jesus gave it to us simply. You might have seen some books titled this or that for dummies. Well, let's say Jesus wrote one for some of us.

Christianity for dummies explains it all.

Thou shalt love the Lord God with all your heart, soul and mind and then love your neighbor as yourself.

He made it simple. Christianity really isn't that hard. Christianity is not a religion. It is a relationship. You and Jesus and the rest of us being friends and treating each other accordingly.

Let's get to it, y'all.

God loves you, and so do I.

I Was Ripped Off!

HAVE YOU EVER SAID THIS? Have you ever had something that was rightfully yours taken from you? Possibly, someone broke into your home. Then after shambling through your things, they stole from you and ran away to hide. I am thinking more of the times that we are living in. You cannot turn on a conservative TV station and not hear that the 2020 election was stolen. There is such anger in the streets. Businesses are being torn down. Merchandise is being stolen and the town folks say their town has been stolen. Multiple times a day you can see ad after ad of an insurance company that is to protect you from someone stealing your identity. Has your identity been stolen?

What about your witness for Christ? Has it been stolen, and you don't even know it? Take just a few minutes. Do you remember the day when you heard Jesus calling on your heart? Remember that day you asked Jesus to forgive you for your sins, and you asked the Holy Spirit to come live in your heart. If you do, do you remember the peace and joy that covered your emotions, your soul? The feeling you felt the next time you went to church. Think just for a moment, do you still have that peace? Does your life show off that joy?

If not, you have been ripped off! No, no one broke into your heart, grabbed hold of your peace and joy then ran, taking them with him. No, Satan is sneaky. He uses slow trickery. Satan uses societal pressures, financial challenges, and political fears to steal from you.

Friend, God was ripped off too and is continually being so. Back at creation, the Bible tells us that God created everything out of nothing. He created everything, and He did so for His purpose and His joy. However, Satan came in and once again, through His trickery, stole the hearts of mankind. This situation then went deeper. God's love for mankind is so great, and commitment to you and me so sincere, that He sent Jesus to die on a cross to pay for our crimes. Jesus did this so if we choose Him, we will be able to stand before God without shame or guilt. Jesus came to get back what was naturally His from the beginning.

We have gone from your items being ripped off to your identity being stolen to you being the very thing that was stolen.

You may not be able to get that thing that was stolen back. You may not be able to correct your identity totally. But what I do know is you can give your heart back to God. Correct the eternal wrong.

Have you given your heart and soul back to God or are you still running and hiding in shame?

God loves you, and so do I.

Living Through the Pain

FRIENDS,

I have been diagnosed with a disorder. A disorder that leaves me in some level of pain 24 hours a day. The disorder also blesses you with, what the doctor's call "a flare up."

A flare up is when something inside of you has twisted or knotted up right against your spinal cord. It obstructs the natural order of your spinal cord, and you find yourself in intense pain. Your mind feels like there is so much pressure inside your skull that it is about to explode. Your back, waist, and legs are in such pain you pray someone would come and cut it out of you. The flare ups can come several times a day, week, or month. You are never sure when they will attack. However, you can be sure they will!

You and I can draw all kinds of similarities from this story. Possibly similar facts could even be applied to a marriage, relationship, or your own agonies that you may be fighting. Possibly you too have been going through some indescribable pain whereby in the midst of life you get hit with flare ups so bad you just wish it would all end.

Well, I have some good news for you! Romans 8:28 tells me that God is in control of all things. Not some things, not only when you let him, not when the Devil's not looking, but all things, all the time!

Since God is in control of all things, and you and I are his children, the Bible says that He will make everything we are going through turn out for good.

One other thing, God is going to get the glory out of every situation that we are going through. What we must remember is it will be in God's timing.

You may have a situation in your life, or you may be living through something that is horrible right now. Remember if you are a child of God, and your Father has your back. He is watching out for you. Yes, it is hard, but Jesus said He has suffered in all like manner.

Some of us have pain and trouble when we must exercise. We know we must go through that pain to get to our objective. That horrible thing that you are going through you must go through it to get to your objective in Christ.

Jesus did give us a way to lighten our load. When I am on the treadmill and am feeling that pain, I turn on the TV or radio. As long as I concentrate on that tv or radio, it lightens my painful effort. Similarly, Jesus said we are to "set our eyes on things above," and He will give us all we need in Christ. If we will just look to Jesus, who understands our pain, He will help us through it and see to it that it will work out for our good.

God loves you, and so do I.

How Foolish Are You?

FOOLISH MISTAKES COME IN MANY shapes and sizes. Foolish mistakes come in all forms and from all directions. The ones chosen here are the ones followed by forgiveness. Forgiveness vs punishment. Two different sides of an extremely hard life.

A mistake was made and forgiveness, although asked for many times over, is never given.

Or a mistake was made, and you can't forgive yourself. This may be the greatest mistake ever!

That would be the greatest form of punishment!

You are one of a kind, beautiful in all ways. You are a magnificent paradox.

Gorgeous but with a few rough edges, incredibly smart, but you make silly mistakes. You are human. You are becoming who you already are in Jesus Christ.

God loves you. You need to love you. I do.

A Bottle and a Bucket

I AM NOT SURE THE time, but I know it was too early for anyone to begin happy hour. Stopping by the VFW, I just wanted to say hello to a few of our greatest generation. It's funny to me that all the guys ask me to stop calling them that. Maybe I do it to aggravate them, or maybe I say it out of the deepest respect for them and the rest of that generation who stood for something. I hung my hat up and said hello to Handy, my friend behind the bar. They called him that because he only has one hand. The other he lost during a fight when a Nazi threw a hand grenade at him and his platoon. Handy saw it was coming and caught it in mid-air. He started to throw it back when it went off a foot or two away from his hand. Turning to my left, there was a table with five fellas playing dominos. They had one bottle of booze each. As Handy gave me a cup of coffee, I asked him who they were. Handy just said, "Regulars. Every morning, about this time, they come in, tip their hat, and ask for their regular. After I give it to them, they head over to that table and play dominos, each one taking his turn telling enough lies about his life to fill a bucket.

Taking hold of the hottest cup of coffee in town, I headed over and grabbed a chair close to those fellas. I figured I would introduce myself if I got the chance. If not, at least I would get the chance to hear some stories while I drank my coffee. Tilting my chair back a bit against the wall and taking a sip of my drink, one of the old boys turned and said howdy. He said Sergeant Fred Hostels was his name, though all his friends just call him Sarge.

"Sarge," I said, "what's up with you and your friends meeting here day after day drinking and telling these stories?"

Sarge said, "Son, well it is like this: there was a day not too far back when folks had it bad. I mean really bad. Everyone was called to take a stand. A stand not just for our country but in a way, we were asked to take a stand for ourselves. You see Japan had just bombed us, and my friends and I saw a chance to be someone. So, we volunteered. It was not easy. We had to fight for our lives on many occasions. It seemed like with each bullet hole or wound of one kind or another we were promoted up through the ranks. It was then we began to feel like we were somebody. The higher in rank the more responsibilities and the more we were looked up too.

"Those days are gone now though. We don't have our men to order around. There is no planning or purpose to our daily lives. It has come down to the adrenaline that runs through our veins when we hear someone call our names. It is not much, but just to hear you say Sarge brings back memories."

"Memories? Sarge, life has so much more to give. It does not matter what your age is. Are you and your buddies Christians?"

He looked me straight in the eye and said, "Son, I would not be here if it was not for my faith in Jesus Christ. *He* pulled me through on so many occasions."

"Well, sir, your leader still has orders for you." He stopped, and I said, "Sarge, there is a whole generation of children that we are losing. We are losing them to drugs, lack of purpose, and fear. They don't see a purpose for themselves, so out of fear they are turning to drugs or something just as bad that takes them away from living this wonderful life God has given them, and they enter a zone where no one can talk to them nor reach them. They are dying without a purpose and worse, without Christ. Sarge, will you and your friends help?"

Friends, we are losing our children. Paul tells us how each of the older generation needs to teach the younger. Paul knew that by doing so it would not only help the younger by giving them purpose, and it would further teach them not to make the mistakes of previous generations. It also would help the older so that as they grew into their final years, they knew they had a very important purpose.

Sarge, don't you see you are needed in the worst way? Paul told the Corinthian church to go and comfort others even with the comfort you have received. Help us help this generation by filling the emptiness inside them. Help them learn trade or give them the edification to look forward to tomorrow. Sarge, Jesus is asking you to love these children the way he loves you.

Folks, God loves you, and so do I.

Living in Pain

TO ALL OF YOU, WHO like me, are living in daily physical pain. How are you making it?

Life's road you seem to be traveling on, does it have a lot of pits, bends and curves that do nothing but add to the stress in your pain?

Is it a hard and bumpy road? Each time you hit a bump does it make the pain worse? These days, does it seem that even the wind hurts?

I remember when I was young my pop saying the phrase, "You guys do not have it bad." Or "back in my day" and then as if to confuse matters, "Back in the good old days." Obviously, I was not there but I do know how hard life is today. Between marriage, the kids, all the kids' needs, bills, and if those were not enough to drive a cowboy off a ridge, I had the Ranch. Horses, cattle, hay, and keeping the equipment up. The cost far outweighed the money coming in.

As for me, the physical pain is still there, it just doesn't hurt as much. I gave away all the stress that I carried. I gave it to Him. I found the Great Physician. He has shown me a way that brings comfort even on the worst days. The Physician told me of two roads folks seem to be walking on. One He called the Wide Road. I only guessed he called it that because the number of folks on it was so great. However, the other is the Small Road. The Small Road is the road where people are moving forward at a steady pace. That is the one I took. Yes, I hurt daily. When I feel pain, some days worse than others, it only serves me as a reminder where this small road is taking me. For in the near future, I will have a body that never hurts. That day, I will be able to jump, run, and kneel without pain. I know I will be kneeling a lot. Because I will be kneeling before Jesus, thanking Him for all He has done.

God loves you, and so do I.

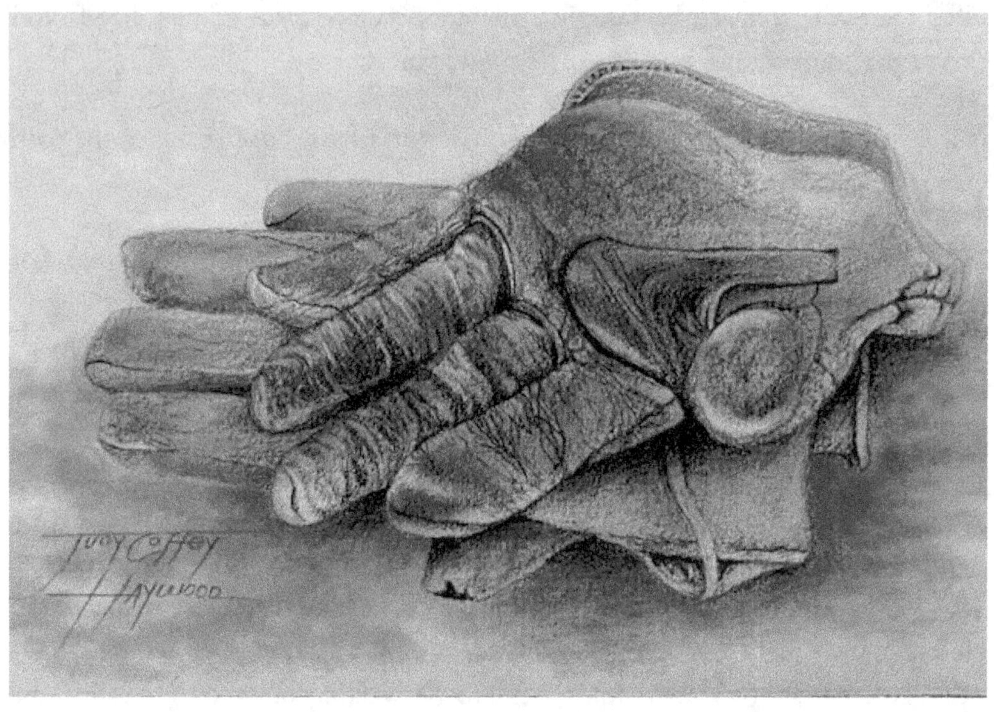

Homes Without a Cowboy

HAVE YOU EVER HAD ONE of those days? You know when you finish up a job that you were dreading? Maybe it was at school, on the job, or, heck, just out here in the back pasture. Well, recently, I had my day. You see, I had been putting off this back pasture for some time. The pasture needed mowing and then plowing and plowing again. Boy, I am here to tell ya it was a mess. Now here it was, the first of the year, and it was going to need its first of the year rain. Turning around, I got that feeling; I guess anyone would, a job well done. That feeling of "I'm glad it's over but look at it, and I did it all myself."

Getting things finished outside is one thing for this cowboy, but once inside the house, there is a new sheriff with a whole new set of rules. I better not bring any of the dirt inside her house or on her clean floors. My boots stay outside the doors, and the clothes, well, I usually drop them in the washtub. Then I run off to clean myself before I can even expect to get a hug much less a kiss or a "how was your day, darling." She keeps a tight hold of the reins around this cowboy's camp. Then, on the same token, the love she shows is like no other.

That particular evening, my bride had fixed a wonderful pot roast. So, we sat on down to a hardy meal. Afterwards with a hot cup of coffee, we relaxed by the fire. It was there that we both enjoyed each other's company and talked about the hardships and joys of our day. When telling me about her day, my bride shared with me how, after she had hooked up our horse team to the buggy, she went by and picked up a dear friend Betty for their monthly grocery run. My bride is all about buggy pooling. You save on hay and wear and tear on the horses. She went on to tell me that once there, Betty pointed out the new employee at the grocery store.

My bride shared with me that the employee was a fine young man and all the talk of the town. She said that he was the hardest worker and so polite. While a couple of the ladies were standing over in the bread aisle, they noticed him run to the aid of an elderly customer. It seemed that the customer was a gentleman who, while exiting the store, tried to get a grip on his walking stick at the same time as his bag full of groceries, and he bumped into an armchair. Then everything he had just purchased fell out of his bag and rolled into the road. Without a word, the young man dropped what he was doing and ran to the gentleman's aide. Each of the women were amazed by his strong character.

I have seen and heard of too many single parents trying to raise children on their own. When asked, sure, some will tell you that they are doing fine. However, would it be better or easier if they had their spouse to help? These young sprouts need both their folks to learn from. They must receive the different kinds of love and learning that comes from their father and mother. Without it, they go through life with a hole in the heart. I am told some feel it like an emptiness and a yearning that they can never fill.

Scripture plainly teaches us that we have an obligation to love our children and to teach in the ways that we know. That includes discipline. Too many parents, whether they are together or not, seem to have forgotten that. God specifically said to discipline our children.

To discipline your children properly is just one more way of showing your children your love. As for you homeless cowgirls and cowboys, remember your little ones. It is not too late. Saddle up, round them up, love them up, and let them know wherever you are they can always call home.

God loves you, and so do I.

A Not at Home Feeling

THERE HAS ALWAYS BEEN A feeling, even a knowledge, that we are not home. We have a belief that our home, our true home, is not here. Further, we believe that our home is being built, and once we get there, it is going to be awesome. It will be more than we can ever imagine. Once home, there will be peace.

Having said that, while we are here, there was a day that we felt, yes even knew that living in our country we were safe and in a place that we called home. We knew enough people of similar belief that it brought peace.

Nowadays that is not true! We are no longer the home team. We have become the visiting team. It has become harder to confess our beliefs. The other team has gotten good at seeking out and ridiculing anyone who believes that Jesus is Lord. To stand in the marketplace and say aloud that you believe in Jesus Christ as your savior is hard to imagine. At the office and in a meeting, to confess your faith seems so out of place.

Yet, Jesus said if you are not willing to confess me before men Jesus will not confess you before His Father.

Romans 10:9 says that if you will believe in your heart and confess Jesus is Lord you shall be saved!

Whose team are you on?

Emanuel! Yes! Literally, God is living with us! Think about that. God chose to live among all of us. God has chosen to live with all the cheating, lying, dirty people. God is not just my God, but He is yours too. He is revealing Himself to each of us differently at different times. To one man He was the bread of life, to another He was a lamb, to another He is the Word or a man. Yet, to some of us, He just is not real. We must tell them that God is the good News.

I bet I have 3 people a week calling me on the phone saying, "Have you heard the good news?" Then, they want to sell me something.

I have news for each of them. The only sure thing, the only true good news, is God came to live with us as Jesus.

God loves you, and so do I.

Stay in Your Home

I WROTE A PIECE A few years ago entitled, "Stay in Your Own Lane." Someone on TV said those words, and when I heard it, the memories came back. Stay in your own lane.

Back on the ranch we had, as most rural towns, thin roads. Maybe the trees grew a little close. Their branches may have hung over the bar ditch and over the edge of the road. When that happens, boy howdy, that will make a thin driving space.

Well, on this one particular day, as we left the ranch and headed into town, we seemed to always drive right down the center of that road. It was like we were afraid our vehicles would get scratched on one side of the other. What tickles me is if that old rusty truck got a scratch, it would have been an improvement. The challenges came in when as we were heading towards town, someone else who had already been to town was heading home. That thin road always seemed a little thinner as that truck coming at me grew closer.

Life sometimes is that-a-way. You know, a thin road with two folks seemingly heading straight at each other. You just know there is going to be a crash. When you will just give each other a little room, the only thing you might feel is a gentle breeze made by those passing by.

I wonder what stories you have when applying the 'stay in your own lane' principle? Husbands, keep your eyes seeking only your wives and not to covet your neighbors. Wives seek to build up your husbands because you should be his number one cheerleader. Teens, know when to stay quiet or just respect your parents to keep peace in the home. Oh, I'm sure you can easily come up with some fun stories.

Put a smile on your face and know God loves you, and so do I.

Good Morning, World

NEW YEAR'S DAY CAN BE, for each of you, a very exciting day! One year, my buddy Tom was asked about what his new year's resolution was. After a moment, Tom realized that he had a choice to make. No one could force him to say one thing or another. He got to choose what his goal was going to be for this year.

Scripture shows us of a very distinct power and privilege God gave each of us.

God gave you and me free will. That power starts with the very ability to choose salvation and spend eternity with God or spend eternity in total damnation in Hell's flames. Then this free will touches the beginning of each day as we choose what kind of day we are going to have. That's right! Each of us has the power and ability to choose the kind of day we will have.

If you are facing a very hard day, you can choose how you will approach each challenge. You can choose to have a heart of joy knowing Christ is in control, and He loves each of us. God has promised that no matter the challenge, He will make the outcome work for our betterment.

This new year can be the best year you have ever had. It all starts with the choice. You can be like Tom, free to choose. Your first choice could be to accept Jesus as your Savior. If so, you can choose to let go and let God. He promised you and me an abundant life. Let's choose to start living it!

God loves you, and so do I.

Paradox: A Picture of Today's World

PARADOX! A PICTURE OF TODAY'S world is a paradox.

What is a paradox? Well, all throughout Scripture there are paradoxes. For example, you must die if you want to live. You must die to yourself and accept Jesus as your savior to really live.

On the face of that, it just does not make sense. However, through faith, it is easy to see the joy that will enter every part of your body and life. The Gospel pronounced in Scripture is a paradox. The word *gospel* means "good news." This country needs some good news. Would you like to hear some? Has it been a while for you?

First, let me assure you that coming to Jesus is not all "lollipops and roses". Being a Christian is hard. Accepting Jesus as your Savior does not mean your life will be free of bumps and bruises. It does mean that when you accept Jesus the Holy Spirit will come to live inside of you, and He will make those hard times easier. He will be there to lift you up when you have fallen. The Holy Spirit will give you hope and that will be so much better than the darkness we are hearing today.

A paradox, hear me, if you want joy, if you want to live, die to yourself. Ask God to forgive you of all your wrong ways and sins. Ask Jesus to become your savior and accept His gift. That gift of eternal life cost you nothing, but it cost Him everything. Jesus the eternal God gave up His throne and died an eternal death to pay for yours and all mankind's sins throughout history. He paid for every sin you have done and every sin you will ever do. His blood will cover you if you accept Him as Lord and Savior.

You see, after Jesus died for you and me, He beat Satan and the death Satan offers. Listen to me, everything Satan offers, the occult, horoscopes, Ouija boards all lead to death. After Jesus beat Satan on that 3rd day, He rose from the dead, and He lives today. So, if you will die to yourself, accept Jesus, and begin to live for Him, you will not end up in Hell. Yes, Hell is a real place. As a believer, you will be in Heaven forever.

Paradox: die to live.

God loves you, and so do I.

Don't Need God This Week?

I RECEIVED THIS LETTER.

"It was a Sunday morning, and like every Sunday, after waking and having my coffee, I headed out to feed and check on the herd. My horse, without a kick or a pull back on the reins, rode up to the gate to allow me to open it. Once through, he turned to allow me to secure it shut. We turned, and with a big smile on my face, I gave him a kick and off we ran. Out through the pasture with the cool morning breeze on my face, I turn from side to side counting my cows. What a morning. The sun was just coming across the hills, and the dew was still on the grass. The oats I had planted were up, and it looked like I was going to have quite a harvest. All the hay was up in the barn, and for once in quite a while, I felt like I had it made.

My bride was inside the house getting ready for church. I just don't understand why all that primping is necessary. She comes to me every now and then with those trick questions. Fellas you know the ones: Does this make me look fat? Which dress looks the best? Can't you see I have to get my face on? Guys, you know there is not a right answer. I remember an old cowboy telling me a joke about how another fella asked him, "Have you quit beating your wife?" I mean how do you answer that? If you say yes, then one can take it that you beat your wife. If you say no, then it can be taken that you are still beating her. There is just not an option for you that would never think of beating my wife. Well, here is another situation. I tell my bride regularly that she looks wonderful without any make up. She is never more pretty than when she first woke up. Does she believe me? No, just another situation where you know you're damned if you do and damned if you don't. Ha-ha. Well, while she is primping, I am out checking on the things I do best.

This going to church thing, I am just not sure if there really is a need today. Like I said, the weather is great. The cows are not having any problem calving, and there is plenty of feed in the barn. I don't see the need for it today. After looking the cows over and the fences being up, I guess I better head on back in. In the barn, I unsaddled and walked on up to the house. With a kiss at the door, my bride thanked me for getting back quickly. She said the bathroom was all mine so I could get on my "Sunday going to meeting shirt." Man, things are just going my way.

It was at church that the Pastor put my thoughts in check. His sermon title was "Do you need God during the good days?" I remember him talking about a story Jesus told. He spoke of ten virgins that came together for a wedding. The wedding was at night and each of them brought a lantern. Each lantern had oil and a wick that was lit. Their challenge was that neither of them knew when the groom was coming. Five of the virgins' lanterns were full of oil; the rest had not prepared for a full night of waiting. As the night went on, the unprepared came to the rest and asked if they would share their oil to which the prepared virgins said no. They explained that if the groom waited until real late and they shared their oil, none of them would be there for the wedding. The kick came as the unprepared virgins were out getting oil the groom came and took the prepared five to the wedding feast. The unprepared came later only to see the door was closed. They knocked to come in only to be met with, "Sorry, I do not know you."

Where this all hit home was to think about the virgins all together getting ready for a big hoedown. I mean the weddings were quite a party. I can imagine each of them thinking how much fun they would have. Everything seemed to be great. Then it happened: their oil ran short, and the groom shut the door to the wedding feast.

Even though today seemed perfect, I needed to make sure I was prepared for the feast of the bridegroom. Jesus said that the church was the bride, and He was the groom. One day soon he was going to come and call us to the wedding feast. I surely don't want to be one to have the door shut in my face. Friends, are you prepared?"

God loves you, and so do I.

Life's a River

LIFE IS LIKE A RIVER.
whose waters continue to flow
The water may slam against the rapids.
But the river continues to go.
Some find themselves in troubled waters.
as their river takes a bend
Others look forward to what may be coming.
Because they know it's not the end
A river that flows straight will quickly rush on by
The waters stir no emotion.
or purpose as to why?
But one with troubled waters in store
Should look inside and see.
The Joy that can be found
inside both you and me
If your life flows in troubled water
Take time to give thanks.
Because Joy can be found
right on your river's banks
Jesus is there with a life rope.
wanting to pull you in
He is waiting on you to call His name.

Stay Calm!

THAT'S WHAT I HEAR SO often. Stay calm. You hear things over and over again so many times that does not make it true. We have such turmoil in our lives today.

The world seems to be at war. If a country is not at war, it looks like they could be at any moment. Russia marching, Iran and nuclear weapons, or the U.S. looking so weak under its current administration. Oh, yes, our country is in turmoil. It seems no matter which way the court decides there will be riots in the streets. Our country is fighting from the highest level of government down to our youngest fighting for life itself.

Stay calm they say. I am not sure about you, but most folks I know are in turmoil in their homes. If it is not between you and your spouse, it is between you and your kids. Kids today! Oh my, don't get me started there. Stay calm.

Friends, it is me sharing with you to stay calm. For all of us who have trusted Jesus as our savior. We trusted Him with our eternity. We can trust Him with today. Whatever you are upset about, give it to Jesus.

Now, if you have not trusted Jesus as your savior. You have no hope. Accept Jesus today! He is waiting on you. Let today be your day. Just ask Him to come into your life and save you. He will.

Let's give our trust to the only one who is totally trustworthy. When doing so, staying calm is so much easier.

God loves you, and so do I.

Consider This

WHAT DO YOU STAND FOR?

Do your neighbors know it? Can anyone who sees you tell what that is?

I ask you these questions because it seems to me we have a lot of "wishy-washy" people. They claim they are standing for this thing today, but tomorrow it will be something else. If you seek to find someone who will stand in the center of town and start teaching what they believe in, you will have a hard time finding that person.

People today seem to be swayed by the problems of the moment. If they are being challenged by high bills, they will tell you their answer for the energy crisis at least until they hear something they like better or they may have another problem.

I'll tell you I like a person who will stand for his convictions, who is honest and tries to never lie intentionally. A liar can never be trusted.

What kind of a world would this be if Christians stood tall for their faith? What would happen if Christians were willing to stand on the streets and tell others about Christ, not caring what other people thought about them? What if Christians really believed the Bible? What if as others walked past us at work or play, they just knew we were Christians and if they needed help, we would do our best to help them?

What would happen if you were a Christian and acted like it?

I'll tell you something: I would rather live a life for Jesus and die only to find I was wrong, than to live a life not believing and die and to find out Jesus was right.

God loves you, and so do I.

Thank Them

FRIENDS, I AM SURE THAT most of us when passing a person in a military uniform thank them for their service. Like me, I know each one of you really means it!

Have you given the same extension of gratitude to teachers?

Serving as a teacher is hard service without enough pay. I want to take just a moment and thank all our teachers especially during the time of COVID. I know sometimes you feel as though your work goes on without even as much as a thank you. Then some of you go home and must deal with your own children.

We are here to tell you that you are chosen and blessed by God to be able to do the work that you do. We extend a very large extension of thankfulness for you and pray almighty God will bless you and your family, that He will keep you safe and well and that He will give you wisdom from on high as you teach and instruct our children.

God loves you, and so do I.

Little Things

LIFE CAN GO BY SO fast that we forget to look at the beauty right there in front of us. A plush green meadow, the snow capped mountains, or even the beauty found in the face of a just born child as he smiles for the first time.

This fast-paced life is so full of troubles. Those who work for companies feel overburdened because they are not being paid fairly. Others are being taken advantage of by having to work beyond what should be allowed, so they never have time to spend with their families. Playing ball with your son or baby dolls with your daughter, there is just no time. As you leave to toil through what will be expected of you that day, you might stop to think about the long list of things you wanted to get to. However, you leave once again.

In the Scriptures, as Jesus and His disciples were leaving the temple and walking east down the hill, the sun's light reflected off the gold plate on the stones that made up the temple wall. This day was right after Jesus had told them of His own death. He spoke of how family members will rise up against another. As they walked, the crowd was praising God and Jesus himself. So, life was busy to say the least. It was in all that turmoil one of the disciples stopped and noticed how beautiful the rocks were.

Do you take time to notice beauty even in the small things around you?

If you do not, why not?

If you do, don't forget what has caused that turmoil around you. It is the one who created that beauty and the one that fights against this world. Don't forget Jesus is coming again. He will restore real beauty for us to see.

If you have not accepted Jesus as your savior, why not today? It will be the most beautiful moment you will ever have.

Jesus loves you, and so do I.

Judy Coffey
Haywood

Stuff

AMERICA IS A PLACE WHERE most people have so much. Self-storage buildings are popping up everywhere. Americans are finding that we have so much that we must find a place to store all the *stuff*.

Is it possible that we are starving, and it's our own fault?

Amos, the prophet in Scripture, spoke of a time like this. He said there is coming a time that we will starve. We will seek and not find. Seek what? Truth. God's word.

People have tried to find inner satisfaction in having more and more stuff, and they are not satisfied. People today are reading, listening, and even giving sermons on positive mental attitudes: how to tell yourself to feel good. People have sought as many ways as there are people, and they are not satisfied.

With every person seeking to find it in their own way, you end up with anarchy. Anarchy is total chaos of people without direction.

Does this describe our country today?

Friends, we must come back to God's word. Jesus is the way, the truth, and the life. He is the only thing that can meet our need for peace. The only thing that can fill the emptiness we feel inside.

Ask Jesus to come and fill that hole inside your heart. He will. Ask him today. He is waiting on you.

God loves you, and so do I.

Peace

THOUGHT FOR TODAY: PEACE, I leave with you; my peace I give you. I do not give to you as the world gives. Do not let your hearts be troubled and do not be afraid.

"I am leaving you with a gift—peace of mind and heart. And the peace I give is a gift the world cannot give. So don't be troubled or afraid." John 14:27

Folks, if you have turned on your TV sets the last few nights and watched just a few moments of the news, this verse may have some comfort in your life. The political intensity has entered our workplace and has possibly even entered our homes. Whether you stand on the left or the right, I ask you to get involved only after you have spent time before our Lord Jesus in prayer. Then do as He did. As He led, you too should lead.

Do not take on the fears and hatred of this world. It would be like putting on a heavy coat in the middle of the summertime. It becomes a nuisance to you throughout your day.

Throw it off and put on an attitude of joy. It's your choice.

As you go through your day, reach down inside yourself and find through faith that *peace* that has been given to you. Just reach down and pick it up.

God loves you, and so do I.

Just Close Your Eyes

SO MANY PEOPLE ARE FLAT worn out. They have been waiting on someone to say, "Just close your eyes."

Now is not that time!

When Jesus walked to Gethsemane, taking a couple of His followers with Him, He went on ahead of them to take care of some business. The guys that walked with him were no different than you or me. They were ordinary people. Prior to going ahead, Jesus asked them to pray. He did not ask them to fight a war or to go preach a sermon to hundreds. He did not ask them to go give thousands of dollars away. He just asked them to pray.

After a spell, Jesus came back, and yes, He found them asleep. It was not a time to close their eyes. While Jesus was gone, He was hit with all the sins of mankind. He had finally agreed with the Father to allow Himself to be killed for our sake. He only asked them to pray, but they could not keep from falling asleep.

Friends, I am nobody special. However, I do know we still need to pray. There is a battle going on, and this time it is right before our eyes. People are falling to the left and right. We must stand strong and at the least pray.

It is not a time to shut our eyes. Make yourself aware of what is going on and begin to pray.

God loves you, and so do I.

Thought for Today

I AM NOT CERTAIN IF it is this political season we are in or maybe something more personal in our homes, but it seems to me that there is way too much stress and negativity.

Jesus promised you and me an abundant life. From what I can tell, if we want it, we need to straighten out our attitudes and start setting our sights on Him.

Encourage each other daily, lift one another up, see the beauty in each other's faces, and go enjoy your day, in Jesus's name *amen.*

It all starts with you!

God loves you, and so do I.

The Calf

TO BE A CALF. CAN you imagine? Being formed in your mom's belly and finally your consciousness comes, and you realize you are you. You have it perfect: all your needs are being met. There is so much around you to explore and get to know. But there is a problem: you feel like the world is closing in and you just know you have to get out of there.

So, you begin to push your limits. As you do so, you know that one of two things could happen. First, you could break through the limitations that life has placed on you, and you could finally be free. You could finally do all you wanted to do. You can be your own person, and nothing will be in your way. Or you could die!

Yet, there is that something inside you that just believes you are not meant to be so pressured and confined. You just know you should bust out of that which confines you and you do!

So, you're born! And everything starts all over. You look around you, and in this big new world, you realize you are so small, but you are you. You are somebody. So much to explore so many things you can do. But as life proceeds, you start feeling and seeing the confinements coming against you. You see all your limitations, and the pressure of life begins all over again. As time passes on, you just know you are going to be crushed if you don't bust out of your situations and get free.

Boom, you see a gate has been left cracked open. Some cowboy forgot to close it completely. You just know it is your chance, so you run head down and hit that gate and bust through, and you keep on running. Unknowingly, with all your pressures and addictions and limitations are running along with you.

Now, there you are standing there with nothing familiar around you. You realize that being totally on your own may not be freedom after all.

Then a Cowboy rides up. He swoops you up in his saddle and rides you back. He stands you next to your momma and closes you in the pin. You realize that it is here where freedom was all along. Bound by the safety of someone bigger than you who was looking out for your better good all along.

That someone for you and me is God. He loves you. Accept Jesus as your savior and allow God's peace to come inside.

God loves you, and so do I.

"The Gift"

When I was a child and mom's birthday would arise

Excitement would build with wonder in my eyes.

I would look to my father for help with her gift.

He said anything from me would be loved and my fears would lift.

With my first job a gift I would buy and never try to hide

She knew her reaction was important to my pride.

Her wisdom shone through as the years came and went.

It wasn't so much the gift or the money that I spent.

As a dad with children of my very own

I was starting to realize all the love she had shown.

When her birthday would come, and money was now tight.

It was a card or a call that I had in my sight.

Now that my children are grown and all moved out.

Time has passed and there is much to think about

Now it seems her day sneaks up and before I know it's here.

And I stop and think what a blessing she has been throughout the years.

Once again wonder fills my thoughts and both of my eyes.

I look to my Heavenly Father and He helps me to realize.

Her birthday has been a day of celebration I truly believe.

For my mom is the gift that I was blessed to receive.

God loves you, and so do I.

Out and Running

IT WAS RAINING HARD, AND the clearance was low. The trail seemed to be gone. Rusty was out and on the run.

It was breakout number two. The sheriff was in a quandary. The last time this happened not only was the sheriff's job on the line, but he just knew his deputies had fixed things. Now it was breakout number two from the same inmate. Rusty was well known. He had a hometown reputation. Even as a young boy, Rusty was mean. He stole from the kids when he was in school and lied to everyone he spoke with. This time Rusty had broken the law, and the judge sentenced him to life in jail.

Life in chains. Bound to a task master. Rusty had been sentenced to serve the will of the jailer. Being in jail was not an easy life: you were to pay for the debt you owed by hard labor. Rusty would spend his down time trying to figure out a way he could beat the system. He wanted out to live life his way. He would not have anyone telling him what to do. The first escape allowed him just a night and a bottle of whiskey. This time the sheriff was going to see to it that Rusty was put in the depths of the jail, alone and in chains to have no one and nothing to distract his thoughts. Rusty would spend the rest of his life going over all the wrongs he had done.

On the run, Rusty thought this time he was free, but freedom has a cost. Rusty now would be constantly looking over his shoulder to see if the law was there. Was he free?

Life can be hard enough without the pain and pressure of one's past. You and I can find relief. There is only one way to be free. The cost must be paid. The good news for us all is that the cost has been paid! Jesus paid it all. He paid for all your wrongs, past, present, and future. For you to be free, all you must do is accept His payment. You can be free, and I mean free indeed.

God loves you, and so do I.

Whatever Happened to Folks Feeling Guilty?

YOU KNOW THE FEELING YOU get when you just get away with something you know you should not have done.

I do not hear much of that word nor of the emotion anymore. I did, however, hear a sermon from a lady who reminded us of some small things we need to do.

There is that cart corral in most parking lots for a reason. They exist so you would not feel guilty for not returning it inside the store. Not only do people today not put their carts in the corral, but they also leave them in the parking lot where the cart could damage someone else's car. Do you hear of anyone feeling guilty about that?

What about perfectly healthy people parking in handicapped parking? Or getting more money back from the cashier than they should and instead of feeling guilty folks think God just blessed them.

I pray we all will soften our hearts to hearing God's soft little voice or that nudge that tells us something is wrong.

We have the Christian symbol on our cars and still we speed and cut other cars off.

As a Christian on Sunday, let's act like one throughout the week.

I pray today you have a wonderful day.

God loves you, and so do I.

Seeking Rewards Not Earned

THERE WAS AN OLD COWBOY and his bride settled on some land. For years the Cowboy and his bride worked hard the land until one day they were able to purchase a few head of cattle. Hoping that the cattle would increase in size and number, they sectioned off a portion of their property. Time slowly passed and the Cowboy continued to work his ranch and raise his cattle. Until one day his herd had grown to a point that he knew it was time. Yes, they had finally grown to the point where he could afford to slaughter one. He and his bride decided it would be a good idea to get some help and at the end of the day's work they would throw a big party. So, off they went looking for help to work in their field . To which they explained to every neighbor they found, those who would help would get their just reward at the party at the end of the day. No one came.

Even though the cowboy was saddened he went to work slaughtering the fattened bull and then it was off to the fields. The full day he worked hard in the field until it was dark. When he finally made it home he could barely get inside his own door because of the number of people who were there for a party. As he finally made it indoors he turned to his bride and asked, who are all these people?and where did they all come from? To which his bride explained that all the neighbors that we asked to come help with our work and we would reward them with a party.

I think sometimes this is how our Lord will feel come judgement day. He has given us all work to do. He said the fields are ripe for the harvest. Jesus told us in Matthew that we were to share His Gospel leading people to Salvation and Baptising them in the name of the Father and the Son and the holy Ghost

The commission Jesus gave us was given to us with our free will involved. We could choose to do so as He asked and be blessed accordingly. However, a day was coming. Judgement Day. When every man and woman will be judged for rewards according to their deeds. This is not the judgement of Salvation. That was decided at the cross and whether the person believed in Jesus and who He is. No, this is for crowns and rewards. I am afraid that like the story of the Cowboy and his bride Jesus and the Father will be there wondering who all the people are wanting rewards for work they chose not to do. They are going to have a + big surprise.

There is an ole gospel song I seem to remember as a boy that had a line in it that said, Nobody wants to work in My fields but everyone wants to eat at My table.

God Loves you and so do I

Whose Fault Is It?

BACK AT THE RANCH, IT was a cold winter morning. I am certain that each of the boys were feeling it just like me. It seems the older you get the more your joints feel the blistery cold, and your back remembers the days of hard labor you put it through. This particular morning, as I grabbed my trousers and went to put them on, I would have sworn I heard my knees squeak. Naw, that couldn't have been what I heard. I must just be getting old. So, I reached over for a boot and quickly put it on and then the other. It was getting late, and I did not want the fellas to be waiting on me.

It was Monday. You all know what that means. It's the day we ole fellas meet down at the Diner. We all try to get there early and have a cup or two of coffee while we share the wisdom we have gained over the years. We have come to the conclusion that this is not gossip of any kind, like women do, sounding like a bunch of cackling hens, not at all. We truly only seek to honor God, country, and to boost our own egos along the way.

As I ride through the snow and ice, it's hard to see. I sure am glad my mare knows the way. Now, once I arrived, I don't think there was a voice in the room that was not complaining about one thing or another. We all hung our hats up, and as usual, our little waitress was waiting to bring us our coffee. The Diner only had three tables, so it wasn't like she was really busy. She just liked to give each of us a hard time, and I think we like dishing it right back. As I said, the Diner was small.

Once we all finally got seated and our coffee served, Fred noticed we had a new visitor. He was a little man that seemed to have been deformed from birth. Yet, I am certain he rode a horse to the Diner, and someone said he had a very nice family. I took just a moment and went over and said hello. Without any shame or pause he told me his story of his deformities and of an accident he had not too many years back that broke a few bones in his leg. He told me that it gave him a hitch in his giddyup, but when he speaks to his wife, he likes to think it makes him look kind of sexy.

After our talk, I made it back to the table with the fellas. To which, I was barraged with questions. What happened? How? Let me give you the short story. He was born with those deformities. Then too, he injured his leg in a riding accident just a short while back. He has a great family and a good heart. Then quietly one of the guys asked me, "Preacher, what did he do to deserve all of that?"

I was reminded of the story in Scripture (John 9:2) where Jesus' disciples ask Him, "Who sinned this man or his parents that made this man be born blind?" In the story in Scripture, Jesus and His disciples were walking along when they came upon a blind man. One of Jesus' disciples asked: "Who sinned, this man or his parents, that he was born blind?" From the beginning I guess that is a fair question. We live in a cause-and-effect world: That seems to be drilled into our minds from childhood. We get in trouble as children because we did something wrong. As an ole cowboy, my knees are making strange noises because I have fallen off too many horses. However, you can't apply cause and effect to the love of God. This man was not disabled because of any wrong that anyone had done. Nor was the blind man Jesus and His disciples walked up upon anyone's fault. It was so the works of God should be made obvious through him.

You and I may not have deformities, and therefore, we don't allow God's works to be obviously seen. Due to cause and effect, we work hard to fit into society with the effect of hiding our relationship with God. It's a real shame.

God loves you, and so do I.

Jackie Edwards Standing United

"SO MANY HIDE THEIR CONVICTIONS in Jesus, because of what people might think. What has happened to the pride in being a Christian and loving God? The division in our country is undermining everything. The good news is that God will always prevail, no matter what. God bless those Christians for standing their ground and saying, no more are you taking our values and our morals from us. As we stand united in our faith and love of God, He will bring justice to the world and restore peace and order to our country and lives."

Good advice. In the book of Hebrew 10:25 scripture tells us, "Do not forsake the assembling of the brethren." What the writer meant was that we should continue going to church, going to meetings, and going to fellowship with other Christians so that we can gain strength from being around other Christians. It seems our convictions in our belief in Jesus and his life, death, and resurrection are not like back in my youth when we used to talk a lot about it and seemed to almost be proud of the fact, we were Christians. Now my suggestion would be, we lean on the word of the writer of Hebrew and continue to hang around those with like convictions to strengthen our convictions that we too might hear the word of Christ and share faith with those who do not believe. So, on that one day when he does call us home, many more will come with us because God does love you, and so do I.

Pastor Mark and a dear friend, Jackie Edwards

What's in a Promise?

AS A YOUNG COWBOY DID you ever hang all you had on the promise of a friend? How about all your life's hopes upon a pretty cowgirl that told you she would be yours forever? Boy, I'd be the first to tell you I was guilty of them both.

It feels like yesterday and yet a hundred years ago when one of my best riding buds swore he would not tell my momma something I did wrong. It was not the whipping I received that I am reminded of; it is the broken promise.

Another example is the pain that came as I knew the rest of my life was ruined as Susie Mae broke up with me. Yes, I stuck to my end of the agreement, and she did promise. I just knew that her words were true. However, over the days, hours, or maybe it was minutes to come, other thoughts came to Susie Mae that gave her reason to change her mind. She was the first to break that kind of promise to me. It was that moment that started to change everything about me. I began to listen with an ear of doubt to anyone who used the words, "I promise." Then as more promises came and more were broken, I began to look upon someone speaking those words with a taste of sarcasm.

The emotions are mixed that come as a reward of a promise kept or a promise broken! Those mixed rewards, bad or good, become the basis of life lessons. Other folks are basically no different than you or me. We all tend to grow hard. Even when new flesh is wounded, a callus will grow over time to protect itself. There are those folks who want to act as though some promises were never made as if that would exclude them from receiving any part of its "reward."

For a promise to be made, there are at least two parties involved. There was a promise made that involved millions and had an effect throughout time. It was between God and the children of Israel. Moses led the nation of Israel out of the horrors in Egypt as the promise of God would lead them into the promised land. This promise was to last longer and was larger than any they may have received before. However, the one giving this promise was unlike any that had ever made such a promise before. There were those that did not accept it. There were those who just gave up on God. Then there were those who over time grew weary and decided to make a career out of trying to find their own way. God, who stuck to His side of the promise, did not allow any of that generation to receive the joys of the reward of the promise. God stayed true to His word. He fulfilled His end with the nation of Israel but with those who were not a part of the original generation that the agreement was made. It was their children that God led into the promised land, and they reaped the rewards of God holding to His word.

God has made a promise to you and me, too. He promises us that if we will just believe in his son we will be saved. That is saved from the eternal horrors of the rewards of our sin. There are those that will pretend the promise did not happen. There are those who have or will spend their lives trying to find a way to save themselves. Then finally, there are those who even though we were not part of the original generation we have accepted God at His Word, and we know that we will reap the eternal joys of our reward.

God loves you, and so do I.

A Reason to Smile!

IT HAS BEEN HARD OVER the last few months to find a reason to smile. It would seem most situations only bring stress. The more stress that hits you, the harder it is for anyone to find joy.

I know of folks who have been hit with loss of employment. Then they were hit with Hurricane Ida. How they feel about our current political situation has only added to the feeling that there is no relief!

Maybe your and my life are not drowning quite as fast, but we all can admit at times life is hard. Some would say it is just not fair.

Take a breath! I have some good news. I heard of a neighbor who has started a "Go Fund Me" page to help people in his town. It is his goal to help his neighbors with the damage of Ida on their homes. I heard of a group of teens going around and cleaning lawns for free. Hey! Even the Supreme Court has ruled in favor of life this past week.

What is going on around you? What can you or I do to keep that good old sense of kindness moving? Friends, I would suggest even a smile is contagious.

Let's smile!

God loves you, and so do I.

News Report!

WHEN WAS THE LAST TIME you heard local news? To be honest, I cannot remember when I heard a local newscast. It would seem all news has become national.

The media's definition of news has become reporting on something negative. Therefore, news itself is a reporting of a negative situation that they publicize nationally, and thereby tearing down any moral and encouraging fiber of our country.

The question is why do negative happenings sell news? Why is the public more interested in hearing a negative story than an encouraging story of a local baseball coach helping a child with a disability hit a home run?

We all can use a little good news. I do not know of a person who could not use some encouragement. The Bible tells us all to be a person of encouragement. The word means to build someone up. To help another along our way.

An encouraging word goes a long way.

Let's encourage someone today!

God loves you, and so do I.

Two Words: Bread and Children

Bread.

I noticed how much bread stores have on their shelves today. In most grocery stores you will find white, wheat, butter crust, French, and a lot more. It was not too long ago in our nations' history when a loaf of bread was treasured. You would find bread being served with all meals. It was there to help fill you up because there weren't a whole lot of other things to go around. The family had to eat sparingly. I am sure in some of our pasts that we too remember a day when meals were not so plentiful. Possibly even in some of our homes today, you are having to plan meals around the budget.

Children.

I have noticed over the years that the more that a child has, the more he or she wants. At Christmas, when times were slim, you might have had to make a gift, and it seemed that their appreciation was greater. Then when times were more plentiful, you might have given several gifts, and their attitude would be totally different. I also have noticed, in the plentiful time, that our gifts may even have been played with less than when times were hard and the gifts were few. The same would hold true with the food. With more to offer, the more leftovers we seem to have. Then when the meal is small, it is all eaten.

If you were to look in Matthew 15:21, scripture tells a story of a Canaanite woman who traveled quite a distance to come see Jesus. Being a Canaanite, she would have had a checkered past …possibly not unlike any of us when we came to Christ. In the story, the woman came with a humble heart and a spirit full of faith. How she knew about Jesus we do not know. However, her faith was so strong that He was the Christ and could heal her demon troubled daughter. As the woman began to talk to Jesus, He ignored her at first, and his disciples told Him to tell her to leave. For in their day, a woman did not talk to a man, especially a priest and a Jew. Then, too, she was from Canaan. They were a perverse nation. Jesus did finally answer her by telling her He came for the children of Israel, not for the dogs. It was her reply that was so telling: She said even the dogs get the pieces that fall from the table.

It is here we see that the woman knew basic human nature. The Jews had everything they needed in Christ, and they took Him for granted. The more people that came to love him, the more that came to hate Him. The analogy of their bread was very blunt. They seem to have so much that pieces would fall off the table to the floor, where the dogs would lap them up.

The Canaanite woman's faith was strong, and Jesus saw it. So, he told her that since her faith was so strong, it all would be done as she wanted, and her daughter was immediately healed.

God loves you, and so do I.

"The Good Ole Days"

PERHAPS YOU HAVE SAID THESE words. Maybe in jest, but when said, you had an image in mind. You envisioned a place in time different but, in your mind, better.

Certainly, you have heard grandparents utter those words. They too were thinking of a better time, a simpler time. Possibly you have heard your parents speak of the good old days, of a time when children were better disciplined and more respectful in nature. Perhaps they were thinking of a time when they were younger and had more liberties and freedom.

I remember even Jesus spoke of an earlier time. However, when He brought this time to our remembrance it was not to bring thoughts of endearment. For when Jesus spoke of "the days of Noah," He spoke of a time of immorality, sexual promiscuity, and anarchy. Jesus said when mankind begins to act as in that time, He will come again.

You see, God loves His creation. He will not let His children go through it. Jesus will come and end the world as we know it. He will come to call His children home. Have you noticed within the past year actions of others are very similar to those Biblical days?

Are you ready for Christ's return? Have you accepted the gift of entrance into His family? Have you got the assurance of eternal life? I have got good news. It is there for the asking.

God loves you, and so do I.

A Little Cowboy's Wisdom

DO YOU PLAN WHAT YOU will wear tomorrow?

Do you make sure your clothes match? That the colors blend and that you will look nice?

I have seen some that appear like there was no planning at all! It appears they put on their cleanest dirty shirt. Maybe they rushed and grabbed the closest clothes to them with no thought at all how they would come across to others.

There are those who treat their Spiritual outlook in the same way.

There is no planning as to what they will wear tomorrow. No planning as to how they will come across to others.

When you got up this morning, what type of attitude did you put on?

Did God tell you that your attitude does not look good on you? What do others see when they look at you today?

God loves you, and so do I.

Marriage—A Cowboy's Thoughts

AT EVERY WEDDING THAT I have performed, I cannot remember seeing a bit of sadness. There was joy and happiness throughout the room. There were hands being shook and hugs being given. Yes, marriage, in most cases, is a good thing.

There are other types of marriages that should *never* happen. This marriage is not between two people but between two schools of thought. These two different philosophies of living or faith should never join.

Government and religion

The fathers of our great nation were wise enough to declare the separation of Church and State. They knew there should be a division between the two.

Yet it seems to this ole cowboy that this is not the case today in our world and more specific in our country. The courtship between the two started as far back as the 1960s. The statement "God is Dead" took hold of a whole generation. It left a large group of people without a place to put their faith. The only thing they had left was the government, and it was the government where they began to seek all their basic needs in life: food, clothing, and shelter. They had come to believe the government was to supply these, and personal accountability went out the window.

I believe this courtship has finally turned into a marriage. The government has taken the opportunity that was given through Covid to marry the two schools of thought. Was it a marriage or just a take over? The government, in my way of looking at it, has violently grabbed religion by the throat and demanded compliance. This is a sad day.

Now, not all is forsaken. Like the 1960s and even throughout biblical history there has been a small lineage of those who kept the faith. You can see, reading through scripture, how God kept a true line throughout time. It was through a bloodline that you can read of the true faith in God, and it is through a bloodline that this true faith still exists. The bloodline found in Jesus Christ. Each of us who truly believes and has accepted His sacrificial gift are brought into His family.

There are those that totally disagree with our faith, and there are some that show it through the shedding of blood. They are so troubled that they destroy property and take things they have no right to take.

Jesus told us through scripture that a man cannot serve two masters. Either you will love the one and hate the other or he will hold to one and despise the other.

Friend, where are you today? Jesus is alive, and there are still a large group of us that believe in Him.

Jesus loves you, and it does not matter where you are or where you have been. It does not matter what you have done or not. It doesn't matter what color your skin is. He loves us all equally.

Stand strong in your faith. Do not allow the Government to make you waver. We have to hold true. Jesus will supply all our needs through the riches of God in heaven.

God loves you, and so do I..

Smiling is Contagious

LIFE IS FULL OF SO many possibilities. Just because we did not choose the correct way does not mean we are to stop and die. No! No way! It means we have eliminated one path and have so many possibilities to go. Our challenge is to get up and go! Even if it is only one step at a time, reaching one person at a time.

"Smiling is contagious"

The Lord teaches us in so many ways. Sometimes through mistakes, bad choices, wrong turns, but He never leaves us abandoned. He is always there to get us back on the straight and narrow road back to Him. We grow, become stronger, and learn what our weaknesses are. He allows us to be overcomers and to make victories out of our mistakes and struggles. It takes struggles to appreciate the good in our lives. Overcoming problems builds strength in our resolve to keep moving forward and get back on track. To make it easier on yourself to overcome your trials and storms of life, build an intimate relationship with God. It is incredible how He works when we let Him into our lives. I know all of this because I have experienced it firsthand. It wasn't always easy in the beginning, but the more you study the word of God and pray, the more you receive the supernatural blessings of God. He loves His children so much, and He wants to bless them every day, every minute. It is truly amazing!

All glory be to God!

Visionary?

A LOT OF WOMEN AND children of all ages have trouble seeing this: a father is a visionary, a person that sees the present things in the light of what or where you will be in the future. Dads look at their children in light of what they can become. A visionary!

This ability can be a great source of frustration. Dads leave home for work with the view of where all his efforts will take him, only to come back home to the frustrations of other family members who can't see his vision.

A happy dad is a man who has a family that will follow his leadership and join him in his efforts. A wife, even though equal in every way, will place herself under his leadership. Children are to watch, listen, and learn from their dad. But dad, you too must live by these words. Dads, you have a father too.

A happy visionary dad is a dad that watches, listens, learns, and lets his Heavenly Father show him His way.

God loves you, and so do I.

Weapons? A Thought

THE BATTLE RAGES ON ABOUT "weapons". Who is right and who is wrong? Do we take them away or do we add more? Weapons!

I believe the number one weapon of all mankind is excuses.

What's your excuse?

Do Not Disturb!

I see this every day. Folks walking down the street, at the office, and in the grocery store. I've even seen it as a sign hung around a young clerk's neck. She was in the large hardware store where you would think the salesclerk would be eager to make sure needs are met. There I came to the checkout line, and the clerk turned and looked at me as if to say, "Can't you see? DO NOT DIS-TURB." I just needed to pay for these items.

Then there's those impatient people that race in front of you at the store. They want your parking place. They hit your buggy in the store. And you look at them and say, "Can't you read? DO NOT DISTURB."

What about in the neighborhood or at church? You have your mind on the troubles of the week and a new homeowner in the neighborhood or new member to the church, and you say, "DO NOT DISTURB." All they want is a friend.

Scripture tells us plainly to love others as much as we love ourselves. Driving around with a fish on our car or a cross on a chain around our neck does not bear fruit for Jesus. You and I are here to help and be a benefit to another person.

Let's take down our "DO NOT DISTURB" signs, and let's help those we come in contact with.

God loves you, and so do I.

"Like" What's in a Word?

WE ALL LIKE TO BE liked. Some people are just likable. They are easy to be around and are not controversial. Their ways seem to go with the flow. Then there are people that are just hard to be around. They are opinionated and stubborn. No matter what direction people want to go these people don't.

Now scripture tells us to be in the world and not of the world. We are called to be excellent. We are called to be leaders of honesty and people of integrity. The Bible gives us examples of men of integrity. They knew that we are to live with devotion to Christ and through this they love people. They do unto others as they want done to them.

They are influencers! They are encouragers!

Friends make a difference in your realm of influence. If you are a Christian, act like one!

Being a Christian is sometimes hard. But it is the best way to live. Yes, you will be liked by Christ Jesus.

God loves you, and so do I.

Hide and Seek!

"FAITH IS A GIFT GOD gives you when you earnestly seek Him, accept Him as your Savior, and invite Him into your heart. No one can give it to you but Him, through building a relationship with Him. Faith is a powerful gift that can bless your life beyond measure. It is priceless, giving you strength, hope, and peace! It can cover you in a blanket of protection and healing in the heart, mind, and body. It can increase your trust in God and your belief in His word and works. Seek faith and you will receive a deep abiding strength that guides you through your life. God bless!"

Written by Mrs. Jackie Edwards

Women's Ministry

Should I or Should I Not?

I BELIEVE THAT WHEN A person is touched by Jesus that he has an innate desire to want to help others and be thankful. Now if that is true why are we not seeing more of this in today's time?

In scripture, there is a story about four lepers who came to Jesus to be cleansed. After Jesus healed them, all in the same fashion, with the same results, Jesus gave them instructions to go show themselves to the priest. Because that was the law of the day. However, one of the four came back to give thanks to Jesus, and he was asked where the others were. Why did they not come back?

Has the world placed so many pressures on believers, or has Satan put so much fear in Christians, that we are not willing to stand and do what is right? It was not that long ago when folks reached out to help others in need. We would see a new neighbor move in, and we would take them a meal or a cake as a housewarming gift because we knew they would be very busy unpacking and would be tired. If we saw a storm damage a home, we would take time to go and help either with money or supplies to get that neighbor back on their feet.

Today, I have seen when it is hard for some folks to take just a second and go to a hurting person and wish them a good day. I visited a convenience store this past week and decided to try an experiment. There was a bus that drove up and unloaded a high school sports team. So, when I made my way up to the register, I turned to the boy behind me and said, "You don't know me, and I am not going to tell you who I am, but what I am going to do is pay for your meal. Then I will challenge you to do something nice for someone else." To the best of my knowledge as I left the store, each boy was paying for the boy behind them meal. It proves to me that if you and I will just take a minute and do something nice for someone else, we could start a fire that would roar across this place. Then imagine what would happen if we told someone about Jesus? Wow, the possibilities are endless.

Take the challenge! Do something special for a stranger today. Be their angel.

God Love you and so do I.

Can't You Hear Me?

FRIENDS, THERE IS MORE TO listening than hearing.

I want to challenge you to listen a little closer when you are talking to someone. Look into their eyes and see what they are really trying to say to you. There are folks in your field of influence that trust you, and they want you to not only hear them but listen to what they are trying to say.

It may come down to you asking, "How are you really doing?" From there, all you need to do is shut up and listen.

Today, you can find all types of people. I see some that say these are the end times, and they are honored to be living in the days that Jesus will return. Then I've seen some that are apathetic to it all and nothing seems to bother or excite them. Finally, I've met some that are scared. They are afraid of the political movements of the moment and are worried for their safety. They see the times that the Bible speaks of and in their eyes, it is going to get bad. These people, or people like them, are crying out without saying a thing. Their jobs, family, finances, and even their church are applying pressure on their lives.

Can you hear them? Are you one of them?

Just letting someone talk may save a life.

Take time today and listen.

God loves you, and so do I.

Troubles!

EVERYBODY HAS SOMETHING GOING WRONG in their life. If not today, in the past, and they are still talking about it.

In most any crowd, no matter the size or the place, if one person starts to speak about all his or her troubles there will be a reply. That reply may come in a different form, but its meaning is likened to, "You think your troubles are bad, listen to mine." Then the race is on: who can outdo the other.

All that kind of talk will get you nowhere. Competing over your troubles will only drag you and those who hear down deeper into the hole of depression.

Try something new! The next time you hear someone's list of troubles, answer them back with, "I'm glad you told me. Let's see if there is something I can do to help you."

I promise the more you lift your neighbor, the more you will be lifted up!

God loves you, and so do I.

Why?

IS IT ME? COULD IT be you?

You would have to be blind, deaf, and dumb if you have not seen the insanity that has been going on in our country. Think about the rioting in the streets of our cities. The police were running out of every way possible to win the battle and those causing the destruction had set up their own town right in the center of the city.

People were being murdered, women raped, and babies' bodies ripped apart.

Our people were calling for less police funding, and our borders were opened to everyone who could make it here good or bad. Massive amounts of drugs were ending up on our streets. It was hard to find someone who did not know of a family who had lost a child from those drugs. Blame was being pushed on everyone and everything.

Our government had become so divided, hatred filled the halls of congress. There were even threats of a fist fight on the floor of congress. The press had become so divisive that they were stirring up strong emotions, and our people's sadness turned to anger.

When listening to a newscaster interviewing a congresswoman from New Hampshire on the topic of election results the congresswoman said she had no idea why a certain person lost. She bragged, "New Hampshire is the *most* unchurched people. They are the number one state in the USA that *does* not care about church." Think about that. She bragged that her people were highly educated and did not believe in the teachings of the church. That was not said over drinks in a bar but in a nationally broadcast radio show.

Why?

In our own town, people aren't willing to work anymore. Banks are closing; restaurants can't serve you for lack of employees, and I wonder if the rise in self-service in the stores was influenced by lack of staff. Our national pride is at its lowest. Heck, I don't hear people saying they are proud of much these days. Used to be that folks go to church for peace and comfort. But churches have become so divisive, pastors are leaving their pulpits. Statistics say between 4000 and 5000 a year. Without our faith, where is the sadness and anger supposed to be taken? I'll tell you, people are taking it out on each other.

God told us, "If My people who are called by My name will humble themselves and seek My face I will heal their land."

Why? Have I? Have you?

God loves you, and so do I.

Beyond Imagination!

WOW. WHEN I WAS A child to have heard such a statement, I would have immediately been drawn to Disneyland. Disneyland was a place of joy and ultimate happiness for children as they saw all the characters come to life in a bright array of colors. It was a place where fear ran, and you were safe, safe from the hardships in this world. Beyond imagination.

Wow. Not today. Disney is no longer a safe place. Our government allows children to be used as guinea pigs. Adults are using children as test cases, mutilating their bodies, testing their psyche, and then benefiting financially from the horrors they created.

Today, I heard in a news broadcast that President Biden has sought to eliminate the word parent. Parents, another place that as a child I knew safety, joy, leadership, and love.

Some of you know of the things going on in the world, others will know soon. Such evil things are in the works. Things to destroy the family nucleus. Things to help the government take control and ownership of our children. This will further allow them to do such terrible things. and Jesus will be left out.

Leaving Jesus out of a child's life, now that is beyond imagination. Church, wake up! Friends, believers in Jesus, today is the day we have to do things beyond imagination to get the gospel, the good news of the love of Jesus to parents and children everywhere. Church, we need to encourage Christians to run for office so that they will be able to share Christ in the planning of cities.

This world is changing rapidly. But it is not too late. You are still breathing. So, with you next breath, use it for the glory of God. Start something beyond imagination.

God loves you, and so do I.

One

WHAT IS SO SPECIAL ABOUT one? Do you remember the song of several years back, "One is the loneliest number? One, you and I are one. Standing alone we stand as one." Most people you speak with will tell you that some time in each and every day they feel alone. Just one with no one standing with them. Alone. Maybe the song is correct.

Yet, one is also first. You can't get to two or three without first starting with one. New Years is the first day of the year. It is the first day of the first month of the year. 1-1. It is the starting place of the year.

Do you feel alone on that day? When you think of it do you think of yourself standing alone or do you see that you are at the beginning of something new? A new year, a new life, a new beginning of new choices of new friends of new places and new experiences.

Scripture speaks a lot about one. The Bible tells how God created one man and one woman. It tells of the perfect garden they lived in and how God gave the one man and one woman freedom to make choices on their own. God had created in the center of the garden one tree with the power of eternal life and death and one tree with the knowledge of good and evil. God told the one man and one woman they could eat from any tree in the garden, but they were not to eat from that tree for if they did, they would surely die. The one man and one woman indeed chose to disobey God, and they did eat. It only took one action, one sin, to separate the one man and one woman from the one and only God.

As sad and horrible as that story is, the Bible goes on to tell of the greatest news. It is referred to as the good news. The Bible tells of how great His love is for us. It tells how the one and only true God sent His only son to die on a cross to pay for the sins of mankind and whosoever believes on him shall be saved and have eternal life.

Friend, you are one. You are loved by God. He knows all the wrong you have done. He knows you so well. He knows you by name. He sent His son to die and pay for all those wrongs you did, so if you just believe in Him, He will give you eternal life.

There is one you. One sin is all it took. one God who sent His one son to die for all the sin you have done. If you will believe in Him, today will become the first day of your new eternity.

One is the most exciting number!

God loves you, and so do I.

Merry Christmas

ON CHRISTMAS EVE, CHILDREN EVERYWHERE go to bed with butter-flies in their bellies. They anticipate opening a present come Christmas morning. Parents know tomorrow they will get to see their children's faces shine with joy, and they finally get to open that gift given in love to them. Some will wake up Christmas morning to see gifts laying around that were not there the day before. The joy, the anticipation, the excitement and feeling that will come over your children they will have a hard time explaining. There you as parents will have a front row seat to look into their eyes as it all takes place.

Yet a tear comes to my eye as I remember the parents who will not be home this Christmas Day. The ones who lost their lives in some war somewhere around the world. Those who were awakened by strangers and taken. Along with others who were tortured and lost their lives in the senseless attack by Hamas, those who now are out fighting for the very freedoms we are talking about. Moms and dads thousands of miles away from their children having to dodge bullets for you and me. I stop and say a brief prayer to God for their protection.

I wonder if our Heavenly Father is growing with anticipation knowing the day is coming soon when He will send His Son to come get us and bring us home. The joy, the excitement, the wonder, that will fill our eyes as we get to see Jesus. We will get to see the home He has been preparing for us for over 2000 years and finally the Holy fear that will come over our total being as we stand before the Father God, the creator of all things.

I wonder what emotions he must be feeling. Soon His children will be coming home. The Father must be torn with emotion. It is His desire that everyone be saved. He must be torn knowing He wants us there with Him but just another day another hour or another minute one two or three more will come to accept

His Son Jesus as their savior. Then they will be added to His family when He does bring us home. I cannot even imagine.

As a father, and a grandfather I know how strong my desire is to jump a plane, drive my car and run, just to get every member of my family and bring them home. To hug each one and look upon their face what joy would fill my every being. Me being human, but the Father being God the creator of everything. I know it is not possible for me to grasp what He must be going through.

Friends, this Christmas let's try something new. As you are in your warm homes with your family, your children all around, take time to bless our Heavenly Father. Take a moment and thank Him for Jesus and what Jesus did for you. Thank Him for your salvation and allowing you even with the sin in your life. Thank him for allowing you into His family. Then finally do something to share Jesus with a lost person. Pray the Holy Spirit will guide you and give you the words and then go. Go out and share Jesus, lead a prayer. A prayer for a lost person to come to salvation found only in Jesus Christ. Who knows maybe you will get to see that lost person as he or she accepts Jesus, you will see that joy, the excitement and wonder that comes over their face as they enter life.

God loves you, and so do I.

A Cowboy's Final Prayer

IT SEEMS THAT LIFE AS I have known it is coming to an end. The trails have been growing longer for some time now, and the weight I carry has become almost too heavy to bear. This journey I'm on has taken me to faraway places. I have seen both joys and sorrows too great for me to tell.

People, we have come in and out of our lives and brought joys and burdens that most people could not carry. However, you have been given a strength that could only come from God above. I know now as the years have passed that life as we now know it can't last. If God does not shorten the length of time, people will kill each other off.

Since honoring me with your friendship you opened your life and heart with me. In doing so you told me of your needs.

It was your husband's salvation and the peace in the lives of your children that you shared your innermost longings. Each would help bring peace in your own heart with our Lord. The things you shared showed your devotion in doing whatever it took to have Jesus answer your prayer. Answer your prayers He has truly done. Your husband now knows Christ and in his own way carries on a relationship. Your daughters, grandchildren, and our Lord have now wrapped around each day of your life.

Now both yours and mine He has blessed. Because I, too, have been praying for the same things for you. It is in your happiness I have found a little of my own.

Now Israel is at war. They have started the ground war and the deletion of Hamas who attacked and killed so many of God's people. Russia has made their alliances with North Korea, Iran, China, and Saudi Arabia. The bear has begun its march south. China is seeing what they have waited for 1000s of years to come to pass. I was in the drying up of the Great Euphrates River that they are waiting to miraculously begin their March and so they have begun. Iran began theirs years ago as they would write on every missile and bomb "death to Israel and death to America". All of this is so important. Jesus told us in Matthew 24 that these things must happen as a sign that His return is coming soon.

Prayer, there is one more that I pray. On this Sabbath join me as I pray for Israel and let's pray for the coming of Jesus. Even so, it comes quickly.

God loves you, and so do I.

Pastor Mark Haywood

Crossroads Cowboy Church

Wasilla, Alaska 99654

This Has to *Stop!*

PRESIDENT TRUMP HAS STATED OPENLY many times that it is his opinion that those who have come after him, if not stopped, will come after you. He was and is referring to the persecution that he has been under from the government and legal system. When hearing him make such a broad statement, one's mind writes it off to an emotional push for support.

Then October 7th happened. Israel was attacked. Since this horrific event, anti-Semitism has spread faster than a wildfire in a windstorm. Across the Middle East to Europe, across the vast waters of the oceans and now across our land here in America. Jews are having to hide and even run for their lives just for existing.

James Carville, a very vocal democratic adviser to many Presidents of the United States, is stating that the greatest threat to America is not the communist of China, not even Russia. The greatest threat to America according to James Carvel is Christians.

That's right Christians, believers and followers of Jesus Christ. Followers of the way who teach the sanctity of life and loving one's neighbor. James Carvel has singled out believers.

Friends, what is happening to President Trump must stop. What is happening to our Jewish friends across our country must stop. What has started to come against Christians has to stop. A federal judge has warned Americans that martial law is in the sights of our government to come against each of us. This too, must stop.

A couple weeks back, a national news station warned and compelled everyone to arm themselves and to be ready to protect their families in their homes.

Was President Trump right? This must stop.

God loves you, and so do I.

Your Attention Please!

CROSSROADS COWBOY CHURCH IN WASILLA, Alaska, has been actively fulfilling the commission given to each of us in Matthew 25:35-40. Now we need your help.

The top story with Anchorage, Alaska news was the number of homeless people in need. The story told about the coming cold weather and winter snow and the lack of housing the city had available for the homeless. Anchorage is not the only city having this problem. Every large city in our country is facing the same or something close to it. With the homeless comes food shortages and clothing and the like. It is not just the homeless. People in all socioeconomic groups are feeling the pinch. They live paycheck to paycheck. Then when a child gets sick, or there is some accident, they have nothing left. People of faith, please come together and give. Even if it is a one time offering it will help. If you can join our monthly giving, we will help you.

The wars around the world and the publicizing of people in need has tightened the purse strings of those few people who have a heart for giving to the financial needs groups like CrossRoads Cowboy Church. As you listen to more and more reports about those in need, a fear seeps in and giving stops in fear, you may be next. Friends, I ask you to pray and stand on your faith in Jesus Christ. He will bless you as you give to others.

God loves you, and so do we.

Pastors, Ministers, Rabbis, and All Church Leaders

WHERE ARE THE REAL BELIEVERS?

Where are the Christians that know the power of the Holy Spirit?

Many, many years ago, God asked, "Where are you Adam? I and many others are asking today that very same question.

Where are you man? Do you know what a real man is?

Why do I bring up all these questions? Because we must find humanity, kindness and truth. Remember, "Do unto others as you would have them do unto you"

The News was full of it. So, I ask, are we?

What are you full of? Are you using it to hide behind, hoping Jesus will come and save you from having to do something about all the News is full of?

In Matthew 28, Jesus commanded everyone to share God's Word and we are to do so *"as we go."* Every time you go, you are to share God's Word and baptize the people in the Name of the Father, Son and Holy Spirit.

My message to you today could be much longer. However, I ask you to remember that for the past fifty plus years many of America's Left have worked hard to empty this country of the knowledge and faith in God. Once empty, they used various programs to sweep our country "clean" of the knowledge and the possibility of bringing God back. Back into our schools, our places of business, and our lives.

Note: Jesus told us that once a house has been swept clean, if not filled the demons that left the home will come back with several more and the house or country will be filled again and be much worse than ever before.

Friend, look at our country. Take note of what you are seeing around you. Never has our country been filled with such evil.

Real men and women, Christians, and followers of Torah, greater is He that is in you than He that is in this world. So, stand, take a stand now, start sharing Truth God's Word. Teach and show humanity towards each other and start showing love one for another before it is too late.

God loves you, and so do I.

Christians Reacting

RAINBOW FLAGS, TRANS CHILDREN HOURS, gays being accused, and people are being killed! When you read about this, how does it make you feel? What emotion does the topic bring?

How are we to react? Some of us sit on our morals and do nothing. It is their feeling that it is best to mind your own business. Some say that they should not stir up trouble. Jesus would want us to be kind to one another.

However, there are those that run to the fight, screaming, "You sinner you are going to Hell!" Then the battle rages on. It seems the harder they fight, the worse the other side comes back.

There is a new television campaign "Take the Rainbow back". It is a movement to take the symbol and reason they believe the rainbow was created back. It is our belief God created the rainbow as a sign of His promise never to flood the world again with water. The gay, trans and members of what I have heard lately called the Alphabet soup gang have taken the beauty seen in the rainbow as a sign of joy and love to each other.

How are we Christians to act? What is your belief?

As for me, my position, and teaching is as follows:

I have interviewed people from each of the gay and trans movements. I have interviewed those who have left that movement and come to know Jesus as their savior. After doing so, I have come to this discussion.

Whichever your beliefs, every person needs to know the other has value. Christians, when we have an opportunity to confront those of the gay, trans, and "alphabet groups" we must keep in mind God loves them too. Peter tells it is His will that all should come to the saving grace found in Jesus Christ. God created all mankind and saw it was good. God so loved the world, all men and women, that He sent His only begotten Son to die on a cross so that whoever ever would believe in Him would be saved.

Now, where does it say God loves what they are doing? This is what we should address and not them as a person. In my interview, I found that those who have come out of those groups felt that they were alone. They felt that they never had anyone who loved them and because they were gay that there was no way that they could be forgiven and could never receive the love of Jesus Christ. It was only after they were told Jesus loves them, and in his grace, they could find the free gift of salvation and forgiveness of any sin. It was then they left the sinful lifestyle and became a Christian.

When confronting these people, we must come to them explaining homosexuality is a sin against God while at the same time remembering Paul tells us in Roman 3:23 All have sinned and fallen short. We must remember whether you slip off a cliff or jump, you both are going. Our goal is to win them to salvation and not to see who is going to hell the fastest.

While explaining that all have sinned, share with them Jesus loves them so much, He died on a cross for each of them and us too. Tell them that if they will just confess their sin and according to Romans 10:9 confess with their mouth and believe in their heart that Jesus died and was raised from the dead for them they shall be saved. Explain that the emptiness they feel inside them will be filled with the love of God. This is the gift that awaits them, and it is free to them because Jesus paid the price.

Christians, there is a battle going on, and you sitting on the sideline and not doing anything is, in your own way, showing acceptance of what the other side is doing. They are coming on stronger; they are campaigning that they are now coming after our children.

Christians, we must enter this fight. We must win back what is ours. We must not let them take our children. If you have accepted Jesus as your Lord and Savior, you know Jesus gave it all for you. What are you going to give to Him?

God loves you, and so do I.

Conclusion

IN THE DAY-TO-DAY LIFE OF a Christian cowboy, it is my hope that you have found he is not unlike you or me. Despite the difference in the years and the spaces between us, the cowboy faced struggles and hardships too. The difference was the wisdom that the cowboy found in God's word. There are a couple basic truths established firmly in God's word that he accepted as fact. Everything from this point on is seen with these in mind. The first one being "In the beginning God." The Christian cowboy knows that God was before anything else was created. He knows that God created all things and that He loved His creation. Secondly, it was not God that caused any of the evil nor wrong things that has happened since the creation of the world. It was man that chose to turn from Him that allowed evil to enter the world. and the evil has a name: Satan.

Each of us has been created by God and in His image, having his attributes. We have His desire to create, love, and draw close to others. When God created this world and the people in it, it was his desire to commune with us or to have a satisfying relationship with us. A relationship where we, as well as He, had free will to make decisions and to act on what each of us decided. We could decide to love God and stay near to Him, or we could choose to live on our own power and leave the God we loved. No matter what we decided there would be consequences for our decisions.

A cowboy understands this more than most. These principles play out daily in nature. If the cowboy decides not to prepare the ground for the seed, the seed will not take root. If he chooses not to let the hay dry before he bales, the hay will mold and go bad. Each and every day, the Cowboy sees God at work in His creation. Yet, as much as God loves His creation, so is Satan trying to separate Him from them. It is in the life of the cowboy that you will find one who takes time to look at the beauty in the leaves on the trees and not just complain that the tree is in someone's way. It is the cowboy that takes time to give thanks before starting his day, and even though he has spoken to God throughout the day, it is the cowboy that takes time to thank Him before laying his head down on his bed roll at night.

It is my hope that you have seen that God's word is primary in the cowboy's life. He also knows that God's word is true, and it never changes. At the end of each conflict, you read of in this book, I am sure you saw how relevant the Bible was in helping find the answer. Friends, I hope this little taste of "A Cowboys Wisdom" has enlightened you and brightened your day. As conflicts come, and they are destined too, remember God's word and how much He loves you.

If you are looking to have a little more peace in your life, if your life has taken you down a hard road, try a little of A Cowboy's Wisdom and give God a chance. Read His word the Bible and don't forget to thank Him as you experience peace beyond understanding. Watch your path become clearer as you too become more like the Christian cowboy.

God loves you, and so do I,

Pastor Mark Haywood

Author's Note

I HOPE YOU WERE BLESSED by your reading of this book, and you will consider one or more of the other Books in this series. A Cowboy's Wisdom. As the Pastor I want to thank you for your support for those of you who wish to further contribute to our ministry. Please send your comments and gifts to:

Crossroads Cowboy Church your gift today.

Crossroads Cowboy Church

3872 N Charley Dr.

Wasilla, Alaska 99654

If you chose to use your credit cards

Call us at 918-413-1802

Author Bio

REV. MARK A. HAYWOOD FINISHED his undergraduate studies at Columbia Bible University and his graduate studies at Southwestern Baptist Theological Seminary. Following his formal education, Pastor Mark pastored in traditional churches until the Lord led him to the Cowboy Church Association. It was here that God showed him a unique way of encouraging folks while at the same time teaching biblical principles. Pastor Mark does this by sharing true stories of the modern cowboy life; many involving his deep personal relationship with Jesus Christ. Pastor Mark brings the Bible alive in each devotional tale about the modern cowboys holding onto their faith and traditions.

If you will take Pastor Mark's challenge and read a devotional a day, he believes you will smile a lot more while being drawn closer to our Lord.

Friends, Y'all keep an eye out for Pastor Mark and our Good Lord will have another collection of Cowboy's Wisdom.

"**Go Deeper!** Gain insider access to Mark's inspiring updates, practical resources, and exclusive content when you scan the QR code."

About the Illustrator, Judy Coffey Haywood

FROM CHILDHOOD, MY FATHER AND I shared a passion for Western and Native America history, art, and culture. I had the desire to learn more, even before I discovered my own lineage. Dad introduced me to the West in so many ways, including the Cowboy Hall of Fame, museums, ruins, historical sites, and galleries.

After viewing Remington and Russell, the quintessential western artists, up close, I was hopelessly hooked.

I have no formal training, but instead was blessed with God-given talent, that constantly pushes the limits of my skills and challenges me to create images that move me most: the beautiful water birds of my Southern roots, historical images of warrior chiefs, and North American wildlife. And simple everyday worn western gear.

These subjects feed my desire to show my own personal interpretation of Wild America, past and present.

Being a realist is easy, for detail is my gift, my labor of love. And I am so grateful for what God has given me